at home

FRANCES BORZELLO

at home

THE DOMESTIC INTERIOR IN ART

with 160 color illustrations

Thames & Hudson

For Lucas and Liza

First published in 2006 in hardcover in the United States of America by Thames & Hudson Inc., 500 Fifth Avenue, New York, New York 10110

thamesandhudsonusa.com

Library of Congress Catalog Card Number 2005911286

ISBN-13:   978-0-500-23831-8
ISBN-10:   0-500-23831-6

Printed and bound in Singapore by C.S. Graphics

contents

page 1, **Harold Gilman**
Still Life: Cup and Saucer, c.1914–15

page 2, **Samuel van Hoogstraten**
View Down a Corridor (detail), 1662

page 4, **E.M. Fox**
A Maltese Terrier, a White English Terrier,
Two English Toy Terriers and an African
Grey Parrot in an Interior, 1868

introduction: 1900

Félix Vallotton
Dinner by Lamplight, 1899

Vallotton understood the potential of a room in the way that poets do: not much is needed to set a scene that liberates the imagination. This dramatic painting of a family eating by lamplight is one of a number of pictures from around 1900 where the room is essential to the impression given by the work as a whole.

Opposite: **William Rothenstein**
The Browning Readers, 1900

In his memoirs, Rothenstein recalled that it was at this time, while still a young man, that he started to paint what he called his 'interior' subjects.

Around 1900 a number of paintings appeared on gallery walls that took as their subject the domestic interior. In London, William Rothenstein painted *The Browning Readers*, showing his wife and sister-in-law reading in a simple interior that proclaimed this modern young artist's distaste for the cluttered Victorian decor then favoured by the conventional. In Paris, the Swiss-born artist Félix Vallotton painted *Dinner by Lamplight*, a stylized scene of the safe enclosure of family rituals, and Edouard Vuillard painted *The Chaise Longue*, in which the woman reading the paper is no more than a piece in the jigsaw of the patterned interior that was this artist's signature. In Denmark, Vilhelm Hammershøi painted *Dust Motes Dancing in Sunlight*, a room full of rectangles of light instead of furniture. In America, Edmund C. Tarbell painted *Across the Room*, in which the floor gleaming in the light from the window is as eye-catching as the woman on the sofa.

What all these paintings have in common is a sense of the room as important enough to be treated respectfully on the canvas. Not just a room as a background but a room as necessary to the impression delivered by the picture. These rooms matter. When they contain people, they are about the experience of being indoors, not just a description but a feeling. When they are empty, they are about the special qualities of a room, not architectural or decorative qualities as in earlier centuries, but its pleasures, moods and occasionally its strangeness. What they also have in common is their novelty. Scenes that put so much stress on the domestic interior as the subject – as opposed to the background or surroundings of a painting – were something new for the viewer of the day.

It is only in the last few years that the domestic interior has gained some recognition as a category of its own. A section on the interior and still life was featured in the Royal Academy's *1900: Art at the Crossroads* exhibition in 2000. Edwardian interiors were discussed in the catalogue of the National Gallery of Australia's *The Edwardians: Secrets and Desires* in 2004.[1] While interesting, the brief for these writers did not require them to stand back from the phenomenon and try to place it in the history of art.

This book is an attempt to do just that. My subject is the domestic interior, the site of the private life of dining, sleeping, working and relaxing. Not only has it had a puzzling career in the history of art, it has often been neglected in accounts of that history.

Opposite: **Edouard Vuillard**
The Chaise Longue, 1900

Vuillard's love of pattern and his interest in female lives passed in sedentary activity indoors led to works of surface complexity that rivalled the Japanese printmakers he revered. In this painting the woman is reduced to one shape among many in the patterned interior.

Above left: **Edmund C. Tarbell**
Across the Room, c.1899

Scenes such as this, in which the light on the wood floor must have been as much an inspiration as the woman on the sofa, were something of a novelty for the viewer at the end of the nineteenth century.

Above: **Vilhelm Hammershøi**
Dust Motes Dancing in Sunlight, 1900

There is no story here, not even any furniture. Just a room filled with silence and patterns of sunlight.

1 what is a domestic interior?

Happiness; home; warmth; light. The domestic interior in paintings is a charmed place. What more appealing subject can there be? It conjures up pleasurable visions of families in harmony, light streaming in through windows or radiating out from a lamp, and furniture arranged in the style of earlier centuries.

We search these paintings to find out about ourselves. Not oneself in the singular, but ourselves in the plural. The black-and-white tiled floors of seventeenth-century Dutch interiors, the polished furniture of early nineteenth-century Vienna and the chintz-covered sofas and patterned wallpapers of Impressionist living rooms animate the dry words of history by offering us a way back into the past. Empires rise and fall, wars bring heartbreak and horror, continents and computers are discovered, but these images tell us that through it all, women play the piano, men drink wine and children crawl upon the carpet, that this family inhabited a starkly elegant interior, that one felt at home in clutter. These paintings answer our curiosity about our predecessors in the least taxing way possible, laying out before our eyes the answers to our questions.

It does not matter that many of these rooms are fantasy. We look at these interiors for the same reason we read novels, to increase our understanding of other lives and periods in a pleasurable way. The interior within the frame may be an invention, but like the tale told by the novel it talks about what it means to be human and, like the novel, its reliance on the details of everyday life helps it escape its era and forge a link with our own. But even more than

this, the domestic interior in art reassures us that we are not alone. It confirms our hopes that the family has a life beyond our own. We don't know what happened before we were born. We don't know what happens after we die. But a domestic interior filled with life connects us with humanity, assures us that there are others like us and that we are part of something bigger than ourselves.

It's not just details of lives that these paintings offer us. They also detail the objects that surround these lives. For example, the copper warming pan hanging by the bed of Pieter de Hooch's *A Mother and Child with its Head in her Lap* (1658–60) helps to answer our questions about what things looked like, what our ancestors used. We can see how they sat in society from the hard little chairs arranged round the walls of an eighteenth-century salon or the pools of furniture that encouraged conversation in the nineteenth-century drawing room. This feeling of arrested time must in part explain the power of the interior, as does the pleasure that comes from curiosity aroused and then satisfied.

Rooms are built to our scale, and we understand them, whatever era they are from. We all search interiors for information, whether we are carpet experts searching for evidence of oriental rugs in art, furniture historians looking for stylistic information or set designers curious about the disposition of furniture in a room at a particular time. In the second episode of William Hogarth's *Marriage à-la-Mode: Tête à Tête* (*c*.1743) (see p.30), a green curtain partially covers an indecent painting – its indecency revealed by the naked upturned foot which is all we are allowed to see. This

Johann Zoffany
Sir Lawrence Dundas and his Grandson,
1769–70

Zoffany has used the interior to
provide extra information about
the subject who sits in his London
house, recently remodelled by the
fashionable neoclassical designer
Robert Adam. Dundas was a notable
collector, as the paintings (assembled
from several of his homes) attest.

practice had its parallel on real walls. Hogarth's *Before* and
After (1731) paintings of seduction were kept hidden in this
way in the Fitzwilliam Museum in Cambridge until the
1970s. Johann Zoffany, working in London thirty years later,
clearly felt the sitter's surroundings added to the veracity of
his portraits. All the paintings in his portrait of Sir Lawrence
Dundas with his grandson (1769–70) can be identified, as
can the furniture and objects. The only lie is that the objects
and the art came from several of this great collector's homes
and were assembled for this portrait in a room at his London
house at 19 Arlington Street, which had been recently
remodelled by Robert Adam. The bell pulls which hang on
either side of the fireplace are thought to be the first ones
depicted in art.

It is enough to say the word 'interior' for people to name
their favourites: de Hooch's seventeenth-century paintings
of Dutch homes; the living rooms of Vuillard that slowly
emerge out of his kaleidoscope of coloured shapes; Van
Gogh's bedroom in Arles. Certain biblical scenes take place
in rooms that leave indelible impressions: the young Virgin
Mary receives the Holy Spirit in a home filled with her few
belongings, including a book, a candle, an hourglass, a cloth
and, in Lorenzo Lotto's version, a pet cat spooked by the
presence of the angel, a disruption of the domestic calm.

We all seem to know what is meant by an interior. So
how odd to discover it is not recognized as a category in art-
historical circles. It does not officially exist, in other words.
The 34-volume Grove *Dictionary of Art* includes flowers,
marines, myth, portraits, landscape and history under its
index entry for painting types, but not the interior. Interior
decoration, yes, but not the interior in art. Clearly the
domestic interior in painting is a complex subject. It is not
an acknowledged category and yet, if titles are anything
to go by, artists (or their dealers) believe it exists: the word
interior figures in the titles of a large proportion of Matisse's
work, for example.

With some paintings, of course, there is no doubt: the
canvas shows a room and nothing but a room. But definition
is not just subject matter. Aside from these unproblematic
paintings, what makes a portrait set in a room qualify as an
interior? Why does one painting filled with a family qualify

Jan Vermeer

*A Young Woman Standing at a Virginal, c.*1670

The interior is an elusive category in art, unrecognized before the end of the nineteenth century. Although Vermeer's painting is officially labelled genre, art lovers consistently think of it as an interior. Maybe its atmosphere and pearly light explain this conviction.

Opposite: **Lorenzo Lotto**

*Annunciation, c.*1527

The innovative treatment of this traditional religious theme centres on Lotto's disruption of the domestic interior. The book, the candle and the hourglass are typical visual ingredients of the scene, but the importance given to the peaceful room underlines the intrusion of the Angel Gabriel.

and not another? Are we stuck with special pleading or can we try and make some rules?

This is not a simple process. The definition of what appears on the surface a graspable concept, becomes confusing in closeup. On examination, interiors tend to cross into other territories – portraiture, genre, moral fables or tales from the Bible – so it is intriguing to ask why we so confidently define some of these works as interiors, full as they are of people, incident and moral subtexts.

Perhaps a clue lies in technical factors such as the proportion of room to people: using that as a rule would include de Hooch, who frequently appears on people's lists of interiors, but exclude the rowdy scenes of Jan Steen and David Teniers, which never make it. And yet this proportion theory does not account for everything. I am sure I am not alone in my conviction that there is an abundance of Impressionist interiors. Yet many of the most delightful images I carry in my head turn out on revisiting to be portraits set in minimal interiors. Mme Manet, dressed in white, rests on a white sofa on which a man leans reading (see p.134); Emile Zola sits sideways at a desk with the Japanese images that fascinated him pinned to the wall behind him (see p.92). In both these paintings by Edouard Manet, the ratio of the interior to sitter is much smaller than I remembered, and yet the sense of these people in their own surroundings is overwhelming.

Maybe the key is the care with which an interior is presented. Using this criterion, the detailed interiors of Hogarth qualify while the more sketchily rendered rooms of his Venetian counterpart Pietro Longhi do not. Unlike Hogarth, the inhabitants of Longhi's contemporaneous and superficially similar scenes of Venetian daily life exist in sketchy rooms that seem of little interest to the artist.

Perhaps mood is a defining characteristic in distinguishing an interior from other categories of art. Jan Vermeer is an example of an artist who can make the mood of a painting contribute so strongly to our impression of the work that we feel justified in naming it an interior. Many of his paintings contain a woman in some solitary activity, playing a musical instrument, absorbed in her thoughts. We stare at the woman, we even weave her round with stories if that is our inclination. And yet, when people talk about Vermeer, they use words like mood, or peace and mystery, words that come from the work's overall impact and from the placing of the figure in a carefully composed interior. For example, *A Young Woman Standing at a Virginal* (*c*.1670) is filled with greys, blues and yellows, diffused daylight and a satisfyingly geometric composition.

The domestic interior may not be recognized as a category in art history, yet we pick up on its existence, subconsciously realizing that there is a difference between a painting set in an interior and one where the interior dominates. I think this explains why it sometimes seems simpler to say what an interior is not than what it is. A portrait by Lorenzo Lotto of a sixteenth-century family gathered round a carpet-covered table is not, while his *Annunciation* (*c*.1527), with its wildly spitting arching cat in a vibrating surrounding space, most definitely is.

Like the Marranos in Spain, Jews who publicly converted to Christianity during the Inquisition in the sixteenth century but who held on to their beliefs in private, I see the painters of the interior before 1800 as a minority group within a nation, obstinately carrying on its own traditions on the quiet while the official world remains oblivious. At times of tolerance they venture out, but mostly they keep their heads down, preferring to conform to the rules of the majority – in this case the official categories as named in Grove. I believe that when we claim certain works, particularly pre-nineteenth-century works, as interiors we are recognizing the clues that betray the hand of a member of this minority sensitive to the possibilities of the interior.

This underground subject has many faces, such as the religious interior, the café interior and the workplace interior. This book concentrates on the domestic interior because unlike the more public interiors of cafés, theatres, shops and workplaces it has not received much attention. It is worth considering why this might be.

2 looking for the interior

Until the 1890s, art history is silent on the subject of the domestic interior. The researcher finds herself in a state of constant disappointment as every source she asks for information stares blankly back at her. At first it seemed to conform to the normal patterns of art history. In the fifteenth century, along with landscape and still life, the domestic interior made its first appearance in art as part of something else, the background to religious images or a clue to character and interests in portraiture, put there to reinforce the artist's message.

The genres of painting were born in the seventeenth century when landscape, flower pieces, still life, seascapes and, just to make it confusing, genre, the name given to paintings of incident from everyday life, fought their way out of the background of paintings to become a type of subject, or genre, in their own right.

At the time it looked as though the domestic interior might make the transition. The paintings done in Holland by de Hooch, with their black-and-white tiled floors and peace and quiet, or the rooms in which Gabriel Metsu and Nicolaes Maes placed their characters, show the domestic interior being taken seriously as a subject. Even more dramatic is *View Down a Corridor* (see p.2), painted by the ambitious poet, painter and theorist Samuel van Hoogstraten in 1662, a masterpiece of perspective which shows what we see when we enter the front door of a Dutch home. Probably a fictional construct designed to display his skill at making a two-dimensional surface three dimensional, it is totally convincing, down to the dog in the foreground who appears to sense our presence. A painting like this, and the *View of an Interior (The Slippers)* (1658), in which a bunch of keys in the door leads us into the room beyond, is an optical illusion, first cousin to the extraordinary perspective box he produced in the same period and now a rare and prized possession of the National Gallery in London. Look through

Opposite: **Nicolaes Maes**
*Woman Plucking a Duck, c.*1655–6

The interior is the traditional
site of a woman's life. Here she
exemplifies industry.

Gabriel Metsu
A Woman Seated at a Table and a
*Man Tuning a Violin, c.*1658

In this picture, the woman
represents idleness and perhaps
something even more immoral.

the glass that substitutes for the fourth wall, and you see how the artist has painted the floor and walls as a patchwork of strange angles and discrepant scales; look through the peephole at the side and the bewildering craziness resolves into a Dutch interior familiar from the paintings of the period.

As well as writing on painting, Van Hoogstraten had a teaching studio in Dordrecht from the mid-1650s and one might presume that these activities would have ensured his continuing influence.[1] However, he does not seem to have inspired a stream of followers.

After this brief flowering, and unlike the other genres, the domestic interior died down for another hundred and fifty years. Apart from a few *trompe-l'oeil* paintings, for example letters in a rack, by Wallerant Vaillant in 1658, or preparatory sketches for subject paintings, the domestic interior never has a painting to itself. Theoretically, it was possible for the interior to have emerged as a subject in its own right. But though certain subjects, such as the Annunciation or paintings of the Virgin Mary holding the baby Jesus, are set in domestic interiors and certain biblical stories are always set indoors – the birth of Christ and of John the Baptist, Christ in the house of Martha and Mary – the interior never made the leap to centre stage in the manner of the landscape or the flower piece. Always there as a setting, to create a mood, to inform about the subject of a portrait, to help tell the story in a genre painting, to supply a sense of history, it is a background which tends to remain in the background.

The interior's divergence from the pattern of the other genres, such as seascape or landscape, meant that it was ignored in the literature of art. No seventeenth- or eighteenth-century theorist considered its place in art. No advice was given on how to paint it. For help in getting an interior to look right, artists might look to the rules of perspective, but no art manual discussed how to paint an interior in the way that portraits or landscape were discussed.

The words 'room' and 'chair' appear in the perspective chapter of *The Artists Assistant*, which was first published in 1768, but only in explanations of the intricacies of perspective: 'Abridgement of the Square is the Line where the Diagonals intersect or cross the visual Rays, and must always run parallel to the Base. It is only made where the Sight is limited by a Perpendicular, as the farther end of a Church, Hall, Room &c.' Or 'Accidental Points are those where Objects end in the horizontal Line, but neither in the Points of Sight or Distance, and serve for Streets, Houses, Chairs, Roads, &c, which take different Directions.'[2]

We might expect the interior to be mentioned in the guides to portrait painting that began appearing in the eighteenth century and continued in the nineteenth, since sitters are sometimes shown in rooms. But this is not the case. *The Art of Portrait Painting in Oil Colours,* which first appeared in 1851 and was still going strong in 1887 with the publication of its forty-first edition, concentrates on how to paint the head. Not until page 54 do backgrounds get a mention: 'This background may be a landscape, a passage of garden scenery, or any composition, either entirely open or partially closed by foliage.'[3] The interior is presumably to be found under 'any composition'.

The guide goes even further and forbids detail of any sort: 'We frequently see in genre and historical subjects the accessories so highly finished as to stand out before the figures.…To elaborate these accessories too highly is a common error with beginners; it detracts from the importance of the figure.'[4] And in case his readers have not got the point, the writer returns to it a few pages later: 'In Kitcats [less than half length with hands] and half-lengths where the arms are necessarily introduced, some object, as a chair, or table, or both, may be necessary to account for the pose; but everything should be withheld that does not either assist the composition or relate to the dignity or position of the person represented.'[5] So, detail bad, generalization good, and little encouragement to introduce realistic surroundings.

An idea of the domestic interior's invisibility in standard art theory can be gleaned from the advice given to students at London's Royal Academy from its foundation in the winter of 1768. These lectures present the conventional approach to the western art of the day and could be heard, with local variations, in the national academies that flourished in every country in the eighteenth and nineteenth centuries, as necessary to a nation's artistic sense of itself as excitingly designed art museums are today. Given by

eminent artists, they were high-minded affairs not concerned with practical advice – the tutors in the studio could do that – but concentrated instead on theory and elevated concepts, a little history of art, and an introduction to the best that had ever been done.

This approach was based on the hierarchy of subject matter, with history painting, the name given to serious subjects from the Bible, classics and history, at the top and everything else below it. This hierarchy, which was held in great respect from the mid-seventeenth to the mid-nineteenth century, represented a notion of artistic propriety, a kind of rule book that ensured every subject had its place, not unlike the system that operates in bookshops today where books are sold under headings of mystery, biography, crime. History painting demanded an idealized or generalized style of painting, as Sir Joshua Reynolds, portraitist and first president of the Royal Academy, explained: 'All the objects which are exhibited to our view by nature, upon close examination will be found to have their blemishes and defects.' An artist's duty was to correct nature in order to create 'an abstract idea of their forms more perfect than any one original; and what may seem a paradox, he learns to design naturally by drawing his figures unlike to any one object.'[6]

The artist-lecturers were concerned with passing on a history of the greatest artists of the past, and the depiction of ordinary people going about their small everyday activities had little importance in this scheme where the themes and compositions of the High Renaissance set the tone. Such thinking ensured that the paintings of the seventeenth-century Dutch, the one place where the domestic interior could be found, were rarely mentioned by the lecturers. In the scheme of artistic respectability, the Dutch paintings were seen as flimsy offerings, filled with detail and figures doing nothing of importance. In the eyes of the lecturers, the relationship of these works to fine art was akin to that of drinking songs to opera. It took a long time to recover from Michelangelo's reported dismissal of the Netherlandish artists as painting 'only to deceive the external eye, things that gladden you and of which you cannot speak ill. Their painting is of stuffs, bricks and

Samuel van Hoogstraten
View of an Interior (The Slippers), 1658

A fascination with perspective interiors is a mark of this artist's work. This is an early example of the empty interior, a category that did not reappear until the nineteenth century. As with so many empty rooms, it speaks of its human occupants; here, by means of the empty slippers and the keys that have opened the doors for us.

mortar, the grass of the fields, the shadows of trees, and bridges and rivers, which they call landscapes, and little figures here and there.'[7]

Sir Joshua Reynolds dismissed Dutch genre, even while he admired the qualities that gave rise to it. Dutch orderliness and domesticity were a wonder of the eighteenth century, and the tamed landscape of canals, countryside and well laid-out towns fascinated visitors, including Reynolds, who wrote home in 1781: 'The face of this country is very striking from its being unlike everything else…this country is, I should imagine the most artificial country in the world.'[8] At the same time, he was so concerned with inculcating a passion for history painting in the Royal Academy students that he damned Dutch art with faint praise: 'whether they describe the inside or outside of their houses, we have their own people engaged in their own peculiar occupations; …excellent in their own way; they are only ridiculous when they attempt general history on their own narrow principles, and debase great events by the meanness of their characters.'[9] In other words, an idealized notion of beauty – for which read Renaissance-perfect – was seen as necessary for interpreting the great themes that were held up as role models.

Reynolds understood that detail and individuality were necessary for 'the lower exercises of the art': 'It would be ridiculous for a painter of domestick scenes…or of still life, to say that he despised those qualities which has made the subordinate schools so famous.'[10] It was just that in his view it was not proper for historical painting: 'It is the inferior stile that marks the variety of stuffs.' But for painters of history, 'the cloathing is neither woollen, nor linen, nor silk, sattin, or velvet; it is drapery; it is nothing more.'[11]

As well as labelling 'domestick scenes' inferior, the thinking of the day supported a notion of the purity of the genres. In the early nineteenth century, the artist Henry Fuseli, professor of painting at the Royal Academy, made this clear to the students: 'What has been said of the luxuriance of Poussin's scenery, leads to that intemperate abuse which allots it a great space, a more conspicuous situation, a higher finish and effect than the importance of the subject itself permits – by which unity is destroyed and

it becomes doubtful to what class a work belongs, whether it be a mixture of two or more, or all, whether portrait with architecture, landscape with history.'[12] In other words, Nicolas Poussin was crossing boundaries by including landscape, buildings and people in one work, none of them having pride of place. This is not the way it looks to our eyes, and, since Poussin's work was collected at the time, not by everyone then. But it is an important example of the way conservative eighteenth-century artistic minds ensured that the hierarchy of genres was maintained.

The closest that students ever got to the concept of the interior was in lectures about composition where, under the heading of background, the interior rated a mention as a tool to create a mood or tangible environment. In the early nineteenth century, Fuseli was respectful of the power of a well-chosen background to make a painting speak: 'By the choice and scenery of the back-ground we are frequently enabled to judge how far a painter entered into his subject, whether he understood its nature, to what class it belonged, what impression it was capable of making, what passion it was calculated to rouse.…Sometimes it ought to be negative, entirely subordinate, receding or shrinking into itself, sometimes more positive, it acts, invigourates [*sic*], assists the subject, and claims attention;.…A subject in itself bordering on the usual or common, may become sublime or pathetic by the back-ground alone, and a sublime or pathetic one may become trivial, and uninteresting by it.'[13] The rule of the day was that the main subject matter had to shine and to this end there was an ideal of the balance of figure and background: 'the most effective pictures, have been those where the least subject matter contends with the principal objects, and wherein the forms which divide the portion of the surface unoccupied by the figures, produce agreeable shapes' lectured Thomas Phillips to the students in 1833.[14]

It all adds up to a picture of discouragement. Domestic scenes are inferior; genres are protected species. Too much detail upsets the balance of composition, risks reducing the point of the painting and is only suitable for the lowest classes of art. Until the nineteenth century, this silence about the interior and these barriers to its introduction stopped academically trained artists giving shape to any vision they might have had, or even prevented its formation. If you were an academy student aiming to reach the top by competing for your institution's prizes and medals, there would be no doubt in your mind that it was history painting which had to be mastered. It is a lot to ask of an artist attracted by light falling onto the floor, an appealing group of objects on a table, the colour of walls and fabrics, or the beauty and comfort of light in a dark interior to make a painting out of them when it was not a legitimate subject and when there was no precedent for doing so.

But art does not exist in a vacuum. Theory is not practice. The recipients of an academic training are not the only artists in the world. And the disdain the academic thinkers had for Dutch genre painting was not universal.

When the Protestant middle classes and their corresponding economic power emerged in seventeenth-century Holland, the effect on art was explosive. They did not share the upper-class taste for history painting, they did not have small altars in their homes and they did not want grand portraits of themselves – at least not until towards the century's end when they began to ape their aristocratic betters. They wanted something smaller, more intimate, more related to the lives of which they were so proud.

The Dutch loved paintings. Seventeenth-century visitors to the country were amazed by how many paintings there were and how many people had them in their homes: 'All in generall striving to adorne their houses, especially the street or outer roome, with costly peeces,…yea many tymes blacksmithes, Coblers, etts., will have some picture or other by their Forge and in their stalle.'[15] When the diarist John Evelyn visited Rotterdam in 1641, he reported on the number of paintings on display at the annual fair, 'especially Landscips, and Drolleries, as they call those clownish representations.'[16] Evelyn thought that the appetite for buying paintings came from their cheapness, their availability and the fact that there was a lack of land to buy.

At the heart of Dutch society was the home, the expression of everything good the Dutch believed about themselves. The premium the Dutch placed on the intimacy, privacy and comfort of family life helped encourage the growth of domesticity as an acceptable subject for paintings.

The virtues of cleanliness, godliness, order and a comfortable but modest lifestyle were all expressed in the home and it was the artists' genius to make this visible. The interior entered art through genre painting. Vermeer's soft grey light, the kitchen scenes and amorous encounters of Metsu and Maes in rooms with carpets on the tables and beds in the background, de Hooch's internal vistas from room to room or room to courtyard, have furnished our minds with a type of home that seems forever rooted in reality. So powerful is the vision the Dutch created that we forget that true interior scenes make up a fairly small proportion of their art.

As the eighteenth century progressed, genre painting became more self-confident. The theoretical absence of the interior as a subject in its own right was counterbalanced by the growth of the middle classes and their demand for images of their own lives in the paintings they bought. Their interest in seeing their values, their pleasures and their way of life on canvas provided opportunities for artists who were open to the seductions of the interior to indulge their sensibility. In this way, the middle-class taste for genre encouraged the development of scenes of domesticity. In France in 1728, Jean-Siméon Chardin won a battle to have his quiet paintings of still lifes and the domestic interior accepted by the Académie Royale in Paris, which until then had disparaged such work as lightweight compared to history painting. Towards the end of the century, the appealing rationale of family life popularized by the philosopher Jean-Jacques Rousseau in his novels, *Julie, ou La Nouvelle Héloïse* (1761) and *Emile* (1762), was drawn on by a number of painters, including Jean-Baptiste Greuze and Jean-Honoré Fragonard.[17] Almost all are set inside the home in which mothers adore their babies and their husbands, husbands adore their wives and their babies and everything exhibits the doctrine of separate but equal worlds for men and women, the home as the focus for gentle values, the boy child in the mother's care until the age of seven, the girl until she marries.

As genre painting became more important, it began to challenge the dominance of history painting. Despite the pronouncements of the theorists, most artists of the

Opposite: **Jean-Siméon Chardin**
The Working Mother, 1740

The rise of the middle classes and the
new appreciation of genre painting
went hand in hand in the eighteenth
century. Chardin's ravishing images
of calm domesticity replaced the fine
ideals of history paintings with a quieter
version of morality.

Marguerite Gérard
Bad News, 1804

The taste for genre painting was
well established by the start of the
nineteenth century and was one of
the ways the interior entered art. The
subject matter might be fiction but its
setting was often contemporary and
depicted with some detail.

eighteenth century came no nearer to theoretical ideas than
they did to the royal families of their respective countries.
Many of those who did this kind of work were not the
products of the grand academies. Below the level of
the great stars of their day, most artists operated as craft
workers, producing what their customers wanted. For
every ambitious academy student, there were plenty who
learned from other artists, whose education was limited
to evening attendance at a candlelit life class, and who
benefited neither from foreign travel nor from the high-flown
rhetoric of the theorists. If they wanted to get on, they
found an artist to apprentice themselves to and learned to
paint like him – for it was mostly, but not always, a man.
Marguerite Gérard is typical of this practice, coming from
Grasse to Paris in 1775 to be taught by her brother-in-law
Fragonard. She produced modernized Dutch genre for
French buyers in the form of finely dressed women in
elegant bourgeois interiors, not in the generalized style of
history painting but the individualized one of seventeenth-
century Holland.

One of the interesting phenomena of the eighteenth century was the way theorists ran to catch up with the artistic developments of their day. To develop, a genre needs an artistic and social rationale. Genre painting, an important route for the interior's entry into art, had to wait until the eighteenth century for this to happen. As the received ideas began to be questioned, the more open-minded theorists and critics found ways to deal with this artist- and buyer-driven phenomenon. Looking back, we can see on the one hand the conservatives clinging to the old ideas and on the other the modernists attempting to formulate a rationale for the new types of painting that were finding favour. Even in Holland, the home of genre, it was not until Gerard de Lairesse examined the works of the Dutch genre painters in *Groot Schilderboek* (The Art of Painting) in 1707 that they were recognized in theory. Lairesse had made the connection between what is now known as genre painting (but which he broke down into sections – for example, outdoor scenes, merry companies) and the middle class by arguing that such paintings should meet the moral needs of the bourgeoisie, and this became the standard way of dealing with the new paintings. In mid-century France, when the Académie Royale recognized only two classes of painting, history and all the rest, the critic Diderot argued that Greuze was attempting to introduce moral ideas into his scenes of realism.[18] In other words, he was annexing history to genre in order to justify it.

It is hard to shake received ideas. Arguing for genre to be taken seriously must have been like the early pleas for detective novels to be read as respectfully as they are today. Jean-Etienne Liotard, who painted the ravishing image of the woman reading shown here, was well aware of the way the accepted wisdom could affect how spectators saw and appreciated works of art. 'I have heard painters give judgements on art which were false to the point of being ridiculous. While looking at a collection of Flemish and Dutch paintings of the highest quality and finish…one of the most accomplished painters in Rome once said to me: "I find no merit in any of these pictures"', he wrote in 1781.[19] No doubt Liotard's own choice of minute realism made him feel so strongly on this matter, but it does not deny the truth of the statement.

Liotard's comments are important because they are an attempt to justify a change in taste, an assault on the ideas that 'everyone' accepts. They come at a time when the official history in which the interior has no place and no chance of making its way into the most respected kinds of painting converges with the unofficial history. This chapter began with the absence in the writings of any mention of the domestic interior as a type or genre of art. Even with the development of genre painting, there was still no mention. I think there are two histories of the domestic interior in painting before the nineteenth century. The first history, which has been the subject of this chapter, is the official one and it is silent on the subject. The second, unofficial, history can be constructed from looking at the paintings.

Jean-Etienne Liotard
Marie-Adelaide of France, 1753

Domestic comfort increased during the eighteenth century with smaller and more flexible furniture and new types of upholstery. This unusual image of royalty, depicted in fashionable Turkish dress, shows the dignity of position influenced by the new informality of the middle classes.

3 the secret life of the interior

If we ignore art history and rely on our eyes, it is obvious that there have always been artists who were attracted to interiors. Since their tastes were unsanctioned, the early painters of the interior, like nervous guests at a dinner party, always made sure they did not offend. They followed the rules and only betrayed their individuality when acceptance by the other guests made it safe for them to do so.

The unofficial history – the underground history, if you like – parallels the other one. And although the domestic interior gained strength from the taste of the ever-expanding middle classes, it was there from the Renaissance, showing up in the corners of works that allowed painters so inclined to indulge their pleasure in the sights of the interior.

Despite the fact that the interior had no official existence, some artists managed to slip them into their art, perhaps as a view out of the window or through a door into another room, perhaps as sunlight falling on the floor. The interior often appears in the small themes of art, such as the woman reading by a window, or studying herself in the mirror, or at work by the light of a lamp. It also turns up in the background of reclining nudes or in the surroundings of a portrait.

To qualify as a domestic interior there must be evidence of precise observation on the part of the painter. It is not just any ray of light through a window but a carefully observed effect, as when Vermeer stands a woman by a window in order better to read a letter, a subtle progression of greys on the walls suggesting the puritanical peace of the room. It is not just any half-open door, but a door that offers a glimpse,

as de Hooch understands, into the mysteries of private life. Not just any reflection from a lantern, but a reflection that reveals Hogarth's fascination with the segmented reflection of a lamp on the bedroom ceiling of a house of ill repute in the fifth painting of *Marriage à la Mode* (*c.*1743). In all of these instances, the sensitivity of the treatment betrays the hands of painters as susceptible to the mood and atmosphere of a room as they would be to a landscape or still life.

Artists fascinated by the interior can be detected in the fifteenth century. Before that we have to make do with scanty signs to tell us that the action takes place indoors: the Virgin sits on a chair to nurse the infant Christ or a roof-like structure extends above the head of Jesus in the temple. In these works, beds, tables and walls are a painted shorthand to alert us to the fact that something is happening inside a house, a stable or a temple. The delight in rendering details of an interior begins with the Netherlandish artists who by the fifteenth century are placing their people in more convincing settings.

At the beginning of the history of the interior in art, I would put Jan van Eyck's *Arnolfini Portrait* of 1434 (see p.185), that miracle of early oil painting. The unsmiling couple at its centre makes it officially a portrait, but it is the detailed painting of the room, the solemnity with which the artist endows it and the observation of light as it enters through a window that speak to us across the centuries. All of the possibilities of the interior can be traced back to this painting. On a factual level, it creates an environment and gives information. On an emotional and expressive level, it presents an atmosphere and evokes a mood. On an

Robert Campin Workshop

Virgin and Child in an Interior, before 1432

The meticulously painted details of
this religious image reveal the hand
of an artist attracted to the interior. It
was a characteristic of Netherlandish
artists of this period to use the familiar
objects and surroundings of daily life to
build up a convincing portrait of the
Virgin and Child.

Marinus van Reymerswaele
*Two Tax Gatherers, c.*1540

The disorganized papers and boxes
parallel the grotesque headdresses and
grasping hands of the two tax gatherers
in an early example of an interior
designed to create an emotional reality.

allegorical and symbolic level, it alludes to spiritual matters.
Later artists might refine and expand on them, but it is these
elements, the factual, the emotional and the symbolic that
remain the core.

Most interiors have one or more of these components,
using the light and objects in a room to tell their stories.
The enchanting visualization of the *Virgin and Child in an
Interior* from the Campin workshop before 1432 surrounds
the mother and baby with what we assume are recognizable
elements of the Netherlandish interior of its day: the bowl,
the fire and pile of cloths, one of which lies unfolded on the
Virgin's knees beneath the baby. Such touches of surprising
intimacy in religious works are typical of the artists of
this time and place and show the desire to help the viewer
identify with the religious story through delight in the
familiar sights of daily life. Marinus van Reymerswaele's
Two Tax Gatherers (*c.*1540) is another work that reveals
the hand of an artist who understands that the details of
a room can underscore the message, although he uses the
elements to create an emotional not an everyday reality.
The tumbling boxes and curling ribbons have a Dickensian
life of their own as the artist exaggerates them to suggest
an uncontrolled financial lust. They are as excessive as the
grotesquely elaborate headdresses of the tax gatherers and
as open to our ridicule.

The religious imagery of Renaissance art kept to certain
formulas. The saints are recognizable by their traditional
attributes, so that John the Baptist wears a rough dress
of fur or hide beneath his robes and the various Saint
Catherines are recognizable from their wheel (St Catherine
of Alexandria) or their Dominican habit (St Catherine
of Siena). Artists followed a similar custom when they
painted biblical subjects in a domestic setting. Every item
in a Flemish fifteenth-century interior with the Virgin and
Child resonates with devotion. Every item in an Italian
sixteenth-century Annunciation is there for time-honoured
reasons of tradition. This practice of investing objects
with meaning could achieve great originality. A follower of
Campin makes a visual equivalent of a verbal metaphor in
his *Virgin and Child* of about 1440 when he paints a firescreen
that doubles as a halo behind the head of the Virgin.

Follower of Robert Campin
Virgin and Child Before a Firescreen, c.1440

The Virgin in her peaceful room is
contrasted with the busy life of the
town outside.

The interior then goes underground until the seventeenth century when the Dutch make of it a great artistic creation. As the one-for-one symbolism of the fifteenth-century religious works loosened over time, the possibilities of picture-making expanded. Campin's type of firescreen metaphor was seized on by the Dutch who realized that the surroundings of everyday life could be imbued with a moral subtext as opposed to a strictly religious one. The double meanings that marked the objects in a religious interior were translated by the Dutch little masters into contemporary interiors, which on a visual level enchanted with their realism and on a metaphorical level carried meanings allied to the ethical and religious systems of their day.

These Dutch painters of the interior took its factual, emotional and symbolic powers and expanded them to express the value system of their society. It is difficult to know how the Dutch 'saw' these works, which created a beloved interior type with its carpet-covered tables and daylight filtering in through many-leaded windows. But if preachers talked on Sundays of the virtues of a well-regulated home, we can suppose that the rowdy interiors of Jan Steen were understood as bad even while they entertained, and an image by de Hooch of a servant sweeping would be viewed with approval as a sign that all was well in the nation reflected in the painted scene.

Once the Dutch had offered their interiors to the art world, they were there for the taking, part of the artistic heritage that later painters could adopt, adapt or develop as they wished. In eighteenth-century London, a fascinated Hogarth used them to create what he called the modern moral subject. The six episodes of his *Marriage à-la-Mode* (*c.*1743), which today hang as treasures in London's National Gallery, were originally painted by the canny artist as

William Hogarth
*Marriage à-la-Mode: The Tête à Tête, c.*1743

Hogarth understood the power of the interior to assist his story and all six episodes of this morality tale take place in a variety of interiors. Cupid playing bagpipes above the mantelpiece, the overturned chair and the servant with the bills all signify a household and a marriage in disarray.

templates for sets of engravings to sell as affordable art to the new middle classes.

This cautionary tale of a young couple's road to ruin unfolds in a series of interiors, including an aristocrat's house, two bedrooms and a merchant's house. Looking at them is like watching a play whose set has been designed with an eye to the plot. Every picture tells a story, helped to do so by the pictures on the walls, the furniture, the views outside the window, the condition of the objects and the upkeep of the household. These are paintings in which the interior is integral to the message.

There is something irrepressible about Hogarth's invention in this series. Clues are heaped on clues so there is no way the sorry meaning of the progress of this marriage of an aristocrat's son to a merchant's daughter can be missed. In the second scene, *The Tête à Tête*, the couple sits in attitudes of exhaustion, the dog pulling a woman's hat out of the sprawling husband's pocket, the wife's parted knees hinting at a night of passion with someone not her husband. In case his caricatural brilliance should fail to get across his meaning, the artist sits them in their grand interior with pillars, paintings and huge mantelpiece, an interior financed by the city merchant on his daughter's marriage to a lord. The furnishings of this room symbolize a household in disarray. The chair is knocked over. The painting over the mantelpiece is a cupid playing the famously discordant bagpipes. A servant carries a spike which holds the bills and lifts hand and eyes to heaven at the mounting debts. It is impossible to imagine the impact of this painting without the leading role Hogarth has assigned to the interior. He uses it to paint a fiction and with this series, and the engravings made from it, he expanded the interior's power to help a story on its way.

One way of understanding the domestic interior's journey to acceptance is through the tide of realism that gradually drowned the eighteenth century's trend to generalization. We can follow this through the interior's role in portraiture. Before the eighteenth century, the fact that the subject is placed in an interior is signalled by symbols. Face after face of the rich and royal look down on us surrounded by the statutory props of column, curtain, table

Gilbert Jackson
John Belasyse, Baron Belasyse, 1636

Seventeenth-century portraits tended to a generalized grandeur defined by a pillar and curtain. In this intriguing image, the artist has balanced the statutory pillar with a glimpse of a contemporary domestic interior on the right.

or garden. In the hands of a seventeenth-century master such as Anthony Van Dyck, the huge pillars and curtains pouring like water all over the canvas impart an aristocratic glamour to the sitters. Occasionally, little domestic details creep into the images but they are rare. Gilbert Jackson included the mandatory pillar in his portrait of Baron Belasyse (1636) but also painted an engaging little room in the upper right-hand corner. With its chair, table with red clothing placed upon it, mullioned windows and a female portrait on the wall, it relates more intimately to the sitter than does the column on the left.

Even when the baroque style of pillar and billow was tamed by the eighteenth century, some of its airs and graces were retained. No one has a problem believing that Hogarth has captured the likeness of Captain Thomas Coram in the

William Hogarth
Captain Thomas Coram, 1740

Though Hogarth has captured the
humanity of this sailor-philanthropist,
he sits oddly in the grand portrait
format, which bears no relation
to reality.

portrait of 1740: those short legs that resist all glamorization
prove that. But where was it painted? Is that really his desk?
And was it really placed so close to that giant pillar – which is
part of exactly what? It is less an interior than an assembly of
artefacts chosen to define him: the globe to signify his career
as a shipwright and sailor, the charter of the Foundling
Hospital, which he established, to show his philanthropic
side. The collection of paintings at his home for orphans
and abandoned children, open to visitors on Sundays, was
the first contemporary collection of English art.

And then out of the blue, England threw up a portraitist
who gave the interior an unusually important role in
speaking about his sitters: Arthur Devis. For the first time
we are faced with a room. Not just any room, but a room
that seems as convincing a portrait as the sitters and takes
up a large proportion of the painting. Devis was more of a
jobbing artist than a grandee like Sir Joshua Reynolds. In
his two most successful decades in the 1740s and 1750s, he
based himself in London, travelling out to the provinces to
paint the landed gentry. Perhaps it was Devis's provincial
background that helped him go against the prevailing trend
of the generalized interior. Perhaps he was aware of the
works of the Dutch little masters, some of whom had placed
their portraits in particularized settings. As an artist not
commissioned to paint the huge portraits demanded by the
rich and noble, he was clearly inspired by the conversation
piece, the century's great gift to portraiture, which from the
1730s to the 1780s had families all over Europe crowding
onto the small-scale canvases of this new portrait form, their
comfortable surroundings a way to speak about their wealth
and culture. Whatever the reasons, Devis's work seems
extraordinary in the light of the conventional wisdom of
the day on downplaying the sitter's surroundings. Devis

ignored this, placing his subjects in extensive grounds or grand houses and his paintings are loved for making visible the Georgian interiors of the middle and upper classes.

His miniature worlds of husbands, wives, children and assorted relatives in their drawing rooms have something of the appeal of dolls houses, and we scour them for insights into the tastes and lifestyle of the people who made their homes inside these walls. However, there is a problem. These enchanting images, which have helped to form our vision of the eighteenth-century interior, seem to have been inventions. His stiff little subjects inhabit their grand interiors in their grand clothes, the very image of the well-bred eighteenth-century lifestyle, but research has revealed that when Devis was commissioned to do a portrait, he

Arthur Devis
Mr and Mrs Atherton, c.1743

Devis has brought his couple down to earth by anchoring them in a Georgian interior.

offered the background and the clothes as part of the package. Several women in his portraits share the same blue dress and many of his interiors are surprisingly similar with a wood floor, an Italianate landscape painting on the wall, high and handsome windows and elegant furniture. Devis seems to have perfected a method of offering a template of an elegant Georgian interior, which he then altered to suit the sitter. William Atherton, a former mayor of Devis's home town of Preston, is shown with his wife Lucy, *c.*1743, in a room that has a grand window, sparse but excellent furnishings and an Italianate painting above the fireplace, and which is very close in format to the rooms of other portraits. The narrow path Devis trod between the desired appearance and reality is revealed by the trees seen through the window, since at this time the house stood in a 'network of narrow passages'. The cabinet, however, which has been identified as of local origin, is not found in other paintings and was probably owned by the Athertons.[1]

We are so used to thinking that ideas trickle downwards that it can be easy to overlook the influences going the other way. The informality of the conversation piece is an example of the more relaxed values of the middle classes affecting the higher classes. There is a kind of modesty in some of the portraits made of the rich and royal in the eighteenth century. The German portraitist Johann Zoffany was clearly fascinated by interiors, real ones in his case, and his paintings are still scoured for information today. His gift for exploiting the informality of the conversation piece made him the artist of choice for gatherings of men at the sites of their work or intellectual passions, such as the Society of Dilettanti surrounded by the art of Rome or the academicians in the life room of the Royal Academy in London. The painting of his patron *Queen Charlotte with her Two Eldest Sons* of *c.*1765 shows similar scrutiny applied to a domestic interior. Once you get past the little princes in fancy dress (Frederick as a Turk and George as a Roman warrior) and the young Queen with her hand on a huge dog, we begin to take in the costly carpet and the dressing table swathed in filmy fabric and covered with pots and boxes. Zoffany reveals how important the interior is to this work by trying to show us more than the canvas can logically hold,

opening up the space behind and in front of the picture. He offers a view of the gardens of Buckingham House through the window, an open door and a standing figure, which the viewers can see only with the help of a mirror behind the Queen's head, and a corridor to the right with a wood floor, a vase of flowers on a console table and paintings on the wall. It is a royal portrait of course, and yet it contains an interior that tells us something about the intimate life of the Queen – a kind of eighteenth-century version of *Hello* magazine. This extraordinary painting shows royalty in the new happy-family informality, a domestication of the aristocratic ideal that was replacing the old-fashioned dynastic presentation of the family.

In *The Arnolfini Portrait* we have our iconic early interior. In the hands of the seventeenth-century Dutch artists, we see the expanding artistic possibilities of the domestic interior. In portraits we can trace the growing taste for realistic and individualized surroundings. So why did the domestic interior never make its way into the history of art? The reason must be that the painters tucked the evidence of their interest into the existing genres. Religious art has claimed the Netherlandish rooms of the fifteenth-century Virgin. Moralized Dutch genre painting of the seventeenth century has claimed the interiors of de Hooch and Vermeer. The portrait has claimed the interiors of Devis and Zoffany. Myth has claimed the nude in an interior. With no tradition of the domestic interior as a subject in its own right, with no rationale to encourage it to come out of the closet, with no encouragement to mix the genres in order to come up with something new, painters before the nineteenth century had to indulge their interest under the cover of the existing genres.

By the end of the eighteenth century, the stage was set for all sorts of interesting things to happen in connection with the interior. The rise of the middle classes, the importance of art as a marker of cultural literacy, the new sanctity of the private sphere, all helped bring art down from the high perch of history into a new role of chronicler of everyday life. A new buying public was anxious to see its own situation reflected on canvas and a new kind of art, based on respect for individual detail, was ready to indulge this desire. It is now the interior comes into its own.

Johann Zoffany
Queen Charlotte with her Two Eldest Sons,
*c.*1765

Always interested in presenting his sitters in their own surroundings, Zoffany paints the interior of Buckingham House in as much detail as the Royal Family. As a conversation piece it allowed more informality than was possible in a grand portrait and shows how the relaxed values of the middle classes were affecting those above them.

4 the unpeopled interior

Opposite: **Jacob Alt**
*A Lady at her Writing Desk in a Biedermeier
Sitting Room*, 1821

A successful German watercolour artist
of interiors, Alt gives a sense of the
comfort that marked the homes of the
German, Austrian and Danish middle
and upper classes of the first half of
the nineteenth century in a celebration
of the delights of domesticity after
years of war.

Comte de Clarac
Caroline Murat in the Royal Palace, Naples,
*c.*1808–13

At the start of the nineteenth century,
the wealthy and noble began to
commission watercolour paintings of
their homes. The relaxed pose of the
Queen as she watches her children on
the terrace adds an intimate air to the
grand and fashionable interior.

round 1800, the interior made a claim to be
regarded as a genre in its own right when a fashion
developed among the rich and royal for having
their homes recorded in watercolour. It could be found
particularly but not solely in central Europe and existed at
all levels, from the handsomely bound albums in which rich
and royal families kept pictures of the rooms in their various
palaces, to the work of amateurs chronicling the more
modest surroundings of their families and friends. Some
of these watercolours contain portraits of the people who
lived in the rooms. *Caroline Murat in the Royal Palace, Naples*
(*c.*1808–13) is a watercolour by her children's tutor and
director of the Pompeii excavations, the Comte de Clarac.
The watercolour medium allowed an intimacy that would
never have been permitted in oil, far too permanent a
medium for such informality. It is expressed in this particular
work by the way the artist has domesticated the imposing
neoclassical interior with a view of the Queen as she gazes
out at her children playing on the terrace overlooking the
Bay of Naples.

The decorative-arts authority Charlotte Gere links this
trend to the development of the idea of interior decoration,
a term used for the first time in 1801: 'within less than a
decade the concept of an independent art of "interior
decoration" was established. The depiction of rooms for
their own sake, rather than as a background to a narrative,
anecdotal, or portrait painting, germinated, reached its
fullest flowering, and died within the space of one century.'[1]
For a few decades, until photography made this particular
artistic task redundant, certain artists, particularly Germans
such as Eduard Gaertner and Jacob Alt, made a speciality of
the room portrait. In England, from the 1820s to the 1840s,
William Henry Hunt made a living painting domestic
interiors of all kinds, from rural to aristocratic, in a type
of thickened watercolour.

At the other end of the scale and typical of those who
found this type of work congenial were the amateur women

William Henry Hunt
Interior of a Drawing Room with a Lady at her Writing Desk, c.1840

This painting by Hunt, who made a successful career painting subjects in interiors, illustrates the comfort and importance of the home after 1800.

Opposite: **Jane Maxwell Fordyce**
Elizabeth Anne Fordyce in the Little Sitting Room at Putney, 1796

The fashion for accomplishments at this period encouraged young ladies to take up watercolour painting. A confined lifestyle meant they took their subject matter from their surroundings.

artists. Because of their chaperoned circumstances, women tended to limit their subject matter to their homes and surroundings and as a result the 'anon' responsible for so many of the watercolour rooms of the period is as likely to be female as male. In 1796, Jane Maxwell Fordyce painted Elizabeth Anne Fordyce in the little sitting room at Putney holding up a landscape she had just completed. One of at least four daughters of John Fordyce, a British Member of Parliament, Jane Fordyce has pictured her sister in an Etruscan-style interior with fitted patterned carpets, Hepplewhite Pembroke table and chair, and a neoclassical chimneypiece that supports a disarmingly higgledepiggedly array of books.

Between the professional male artists and amateur females came someone such as Mary Ellen Best who sold her portraits, still lifes and interiors to the inhabitants of York, her native city, and Frankfurt, where she lived for a while and where she met her husband. Best was one of the many semi-professional women painters who were part of an international phenomenon of this period, the product of an improved education that included drawing and painting in a curriculum which had as its goal the making of a middle-class lady. Like many young women of her day, Best was taught flower, animal and portrait painting as part of her education and then, a little more surprisingly, though not so rare an occurrence as one might think, set herself up as an artist after leaving school. Serious about improving her art in order to practise professionally, she compensated for the art school ban on female students by constant drawing and by visiting private collections. Many amateurs learned to paint interiors from books of interior decoration or from country-house guides, but this was not enough for Best. Denied academic credentials, she looked for official approval in other ways and in 1830 won a medal from the Society for the Encouragement of Arts, Manufactures and Commerce (today's Royal Society of Arts) in London for a still life of bottles, bread, jug and apples on a cloth-covered table. From this she progressed to interiors of churches, work places and houses, of which the domestic interiors are the most numerous and, with their everyday detail, the most fascinating. In her list of paintings sold during a stay in

Frankfurt in 1834–5, she names one landscape, six portraits and seven interiors – she actually did call them that. As with so many women who decorously attempted to straddle the amateur-professional divide, a legacy, marriage in 1840, and a new life as a wife and mother of two on the Continent, ended her professional career. Happily for later generations, however, she continued to chronicle her family life, making her a member of that select band of female artists who record their lives in what is tantamount to a visual diary.

These watercolour rooms are the first paintings since Van Hoogstraten that uncompromisingly take as their subject the domestic interior. However, I am unsure of their role in encouraging oil painters to see the artistic possibilities of the interior. Their association with women, amateurism, portraiture and a lightweight medium makes it unlikely that this flurry of interiors advanced the cause. Beloved though they may have been by their owners, and even though some well-known artists produced them, no one ever valued such paintings as art. Oil was the medium for serious art, not watercolour. As portraits, they were only one step up from copying, considered the lowest form of artistic creation since it did not require the use of the intellect and imagination. And they were often done by amateurs and women, which automatically lowered their status. Any respect such paintings earned – like portraits of people – tended to be related to the glamour of the rooms' owners as much as to the pictures' artistic worth.

On the other hand, it is a fact that after centuries in which the interior is hard to find, it suddenly begins to show up in paintings. One piece of evidence that oil painters were beginning to be influenced by these watercolours is offered by Robert Huskisson's painting of *Lord Northwick's Picture Gallery at Thirlestaine House* (c.1846–7). In art-historical terms, it is possible to track its ancestry back to seventeenth-century Flemish paintings of art collections, but nonetheless it brings something new to the type. For one thing, Huskisson's painting is a specific portrait while the Flemish images are generally agreed to be idealized confections of possessions. Huskisson's is also a far more feminized image. In the Flemish paintings, women appear in the paintings on the walls but rarely among the

connoisseurs. Huskisson's idea of including two pretty women and a playful dog to soften the geometry of the neoclassical interior with its frieze and axial view of other rooms is new, evidence of the arrival of cheerful domesticity in even the grandest homes.

Perhaps it is most helpful to see the watercolour room-portraits as a symptom of the new importance of the domestic interior to society and, through society, art. In the journey from the feudal household to the bourgeois home, the layout of homes, from the one room of the poor to the great halls of the grand where the whole household mingled, gave way to boundaries between servant and employer, children and parents and the assorted household activities. By the early seventeenth century in Holland an urban middle class existed of one family to a house, with rooms dedicated to eating, cooking, entertaining and sleeping, and this spread to other countries in the following century. 'In the eighteenth century, the family began to hold society at a distance,' writes the French historian Philippe Aries, 'to push it back beyond a steadily extending zone of private life. The organization of the house altered in conformity with this new desire to keep the world at bay. It became the modern type of house, with rooms which were independent because they opened on to a corridor….It has been said that comfort dates from this period; it was born at the same time as domesticity, privacy and isolation, and it was one of the manifestations of these phenomena.'[2]

Advances in domestic comfort did much to make the interior a more enticing place. Since the end of the eighteenth century, furniture had indeed become more comfortable and new types and styles followed in quick succession. Improvements in upholstery techniques added to the pleasures of such new recreations as novel reading, and lighter, smaller and more adaptable pieces of furniture were invented that could be moved around to suit the owner's will. A new notion of coziness accompanied all this. John Tosh, an academic with an interest in masculinity and the home, describes domesticity as a nineteenth-century invention: 'Its defining attributes are privacy and comfort, separation from the workplace, and the merging of domestic

Mary Ellen Best
Our Dining Room at York, 1838

Watercolour interiors, like this one of the artist's home, offer valuable information on living styles of the day. Best was typical of the semi-professional female watercolourists who were a phenomenon of the period.

Robert Huskisson
Lord Northwick's Picture Gallery at
*Thirlstaine House, c.*1846–7

This painting of a private picture gallery,
with an imposing axial view into the
rooms beyond, shows that the fashion
for watercolour interiors which opened
the century had migrated into the more
serious medium of oil.

space and family members into a single commanding
concept (in English, "home")….One can go further and
say that it was an integral part of modernity: socially it was
inconceivable without large-scale urbanization; culturally
it was one of the most important expressions of that
awareness of individual interiority which had developed
since the Enlightenment.'[3]

These developments helped the domestic interior
become a credible subject for art. Examples of the
unpeopled interior, the purest form the subject can take,
and also its rarest face, began to appear in oil paintings early
in the nineteenth century. Van Hoogstraten aside, the few
pre-nineteenth-century examples tend to be preparatory
studies for more ambitious history paintings. But the new
ideas about privacy and personalizing one's surroundings,
as well as the fashion for recording rooms in watercolours,
encouraged artists to see it as a possible subject. The
conviction that no excuse was needed for an oil painting
beyond the room in front of one's eyes did not take hold
until the century's second half, but there are examples before
1850 that show how important the room had become.

There was one other development that helped bring
the empty interior into oil painting and that was the new
sensibility of the Romantic movement, which valued the
individual and the personal. Much has been written about
the subjectivity of Romantic writers but I think the painters
gave a visual face to the development of private life. We
can see this happening in the early years of the nineteenth
century in the way their living and working spaces become
an important motif, particularly for the artists of central
Europe. I hesitate to call them studios since they display
no hint of the agonies of creation. There is a domestic air
to these paintings that is closer to sitting room than studio.
There is usually an easel, of course, but also a table, a chair,
a canvas, a vase of flowers, and a second frame around
the window. These modest paintings, which radiate peace,
privacy and calm, are by artists who think, who dream and
who value the world they see from their windows. There
is an element of the monk's cell to them, but updated and
softened, with less of the fearful attitude to life and more
of an awareness that the here and now can carry spiritual

Adolph Menzel
The Balcony Room, 1845

Menzel's ravishing oil sketch of the corner of an empty bedroom is as alive as the breeze that swells the curtain. The casually placed chair, open window and clothes strewn on the bed carry the imprint of the absent occupants.

overtones. They are legitimizing and secularizing the solitary, it seems to me.

A different facet of the empty interior can be seen in works done by the German artist Adolph Menzel in the last years of the 1840s. While in his thirties, Menzel made several oil sketches of interiors, some with people in them, some without. Though they appeal to a modern sensibility, it is hard to imagine anyone outside the artist's inner circle wanting these works. These are not finished paintings in an exhibiting sense, as their medium – board or paper – makes clear. They would never have been accepted as completed works of art: their subject matter is too indefinite and slight and their technique, though stunning, far too sketchy for the taste of the time. It is a similar situation to Turner's colour beginnings, those washes of blue and yellow oils that to our dazzled eyes seem to predate Abstract Expressionism. No one would have wanted them when he painted them and it is not surprising that so many were stashed in his studio when he died. However much he may have loved them, however satisfied he was with them, such works could not have been sent out into the art world of his day.

In 1847, Menzel painted *The Bedroom*, a view past his bed and out of the window. Aside from the sketchy treatment, which could have no place in a finished painting of its time, he achieves an extraordinary approximation to visual experience as we sense a mounded bed in the foreground but then find our gaze dragged from the room to the houses outside. He manages to replicate in paint the way we see, as he first guides us to look out of the window and then, through our consciousness of the light hitting the bed cover and the desk, brings us back into the room.

One of the powers of the empty interior is its ability to suggest the human presence, something that Van Hoogstraten, apparently the first to exploit the power of the unpeopled interior to hold its own as a work of art, understood very well. Even though his book of 1678 devoted a great deal of space to explaining the mechanics of perspective, he seems to have been unable, theorist or not, to envisage an interior without a human presence. Sometimes he does this literally: the couple sitting in an alcove by the window whose light brightens the tiles it falls on humanize the *View Down a Corridor*. Sometimes figuratively: as well as being a foreground device to distance the room beyond, the keys in the door of the *View of an Interior* speak of the hand that put them there .

Because of our personal link with rooms, the unpeopled painted interior can carry an extraordinary charge of humanity. In the nineteenth century, artists learned how to exploit the fact that the interior could bear the imprint of people. We are aware of an absence. Or we sense a presence. Open windows, cushions, doors left ajar refer to the person who has just left or is about to enter. It seems to be encoded in the nature of rooms to speak about the human presence, in the way that old costumes in museum display cases give rise to thoughts about those who wore them.

The sense of an invisible human presence, which is the empty interior's particular gift to the visual arts, is evident in Menzel's *Balcony Room* of 1845, another of the group of oil sketches on board. Often used by art historians as an example of Impressionism before its time, the *Balcony Room* presents the viewer with a corner of a room that seems as alive now as when Menzel painted it. More than mere decor, it is a mixture of sensitivity to light, harmonious colours, of peace and the mild air of summer. Somehow Menzel has made this interior breathe. The breeze pushes the gauzy curtain into the room, there are clothes discarded in the open drawer and on the bed. There is a palable human presence in this room, suggested by the bed glimpsed in the mirror, the casually placed chairs that someone has moved, the gilt-framed picture someone has selected to sit above the bed, the window someone has opened. One of the achievements of this small work is to make us feel we are inside the space. We know how quiet it is. We see the the line of light on the chair before the window. We feel the breeze. We look into the mirror. By managing to put our senses to work, Menzel has placed us in the room.

Artists are disobliging creatures who do not always leave us the reasons why they painted particular interiors, but it seems clear in some cases that happiness was the spur for a number of unpeopled interiors in the second half of the

century. Van Gogh transmits his joy in his bedroom at Arles through a living line and pure colours straight from the tube. The towel squirms on its hook by the door, the bed bulges with its sense of self. The engaging joy in simplicity, colour and a cherished place of peace, which has resulted in reproductions hanging on countless walls, was part of the painter's intention: 'In a word, looking at the picture ought to rest the brain, or rather the imagination,' he wrote to his brother Theo in 1888. 'The walls are pale violet. The floor is of red tiles. The wood of the bed and chairs is the yellow of fresh butter, the sheets and pillows very light greenish-citron. The coverlet scarlet. The window green. The toilet table orange, the basin blue. The doors lilac. And that is all – there is nothing in this room with its closed shutters. The broad lines of the furniture must express inviolable rest.'[4] Van Gogh's *Bedroom* (1888) at Arles is a kind of substitute self-portrait, one that shows him at his happiest and most hopeful, with his dream of an artistic community in the south of France intact.

Though also painted out of happiness, Gwen John's *A Corner of the Artist's Room in Paris* (1907–9) offers a different kind of visual experience. Unlike Van Gogh's uninhibited delight in bold colour and strong light, Gwen John transmits her joy in her room through a pale and restricted colour palette that suggests her sensitivity to light and air. Gwen John did this painting of her room in Paris when she was in love with the sculptor Auguste Rodin who had seduced her while she modelled for his monument to James Abbott McNeill Whistler. At this period, within two years of meeting the great sculptor, she was deeply obsessed by him, unaware that he was cooling towards his passionate conquest. Gwen John had moved to this room to please Rodin who had complained about the condition of her previous lodgings, and she loved it: 'what a feeling of contentment my room gives me. I take my meals at the table in the window.…In the evening, my room gives me a quite extraordinary feeling of pleasure.'[5] Like Menzel's painting, Gwen John's room is filled with a human presence. The posy of flowers, and the parasol propped against the pretty wicker chair placed near the window to catch the light, speak of the artist who arranged them in what can only be seen as a

Opposite: Gwen John
A Corner of the Artist's Room in Paris, 1907–9

A small category of uninhabited interiors at this period can be read as sublimated self-portraits. John's delicate treatment of her attic lodgings speaks of her independence – the parasol – and her pleasures – the posy of flowers and the light that enters through the delicate curtains.

Vincent van Gogh
The Bedroom, 1888

This is one of a handful of iconic interiors in the history of art. The bright colours and energetic lines relate to an optimistic time in the artist's life when he was painting with Gauguin in the south of France.

self-portrait of a fulfilled and happy woman. Both this painting and Van Gogh's *Bedroom* communicate their makers' strong feelings for their spaces. In making them, Van Gogh was dreaming of an artistic utopia which he could share with Gauguin, and Gwen John, alone and sexually awakened, was dreaming of Rodin.

An interesting version of the unpeopled room-portrait is that which presents the painter's credo. In *My Favourite Room* (1892), the Belgian James Ensor presents his room to us in the form of a shrine to his art and his beliefs. The layout suggests that we enter as into a sacred place and are stopped, as if in church, by an equivalent to the altar table. A painting of an older professional colleague, the artist Isidore Verheyden, dressed for outdoors in hat, overcoat and cane, watches us enter. The paintings that surround him are by Ensor and include *The Man of Sorrows* (1891), in which Ensor identifies himself with Christ persecuted by critics. There is an unguarded quality about this work, which to my eyes is both private and revealing. Ensor never married and never threw off the outwardly bourgeois trappings depicted in works like this. His escape was in his strange and startling art of masks, skeletons and religion come down to earth. *My Favourite Room* shows him uniting the conventionally bourgeois and the unconventional artistic sides of his life and he kept it for years.

In 1909, Gabriele Münter painted *Bedroom in Murnau*, a night-time portrait of the summer home she had recently bought in the Bavarian village of Murnau. At this period, she and her lover, the Russian artist Vassily Kandinsky, who can be seen reading in bed through the door on the left, one arm up behind his head, were living and breathing art alongside their painter friends Alexei Jawlensky and Marianne Werefkin. The painting sings with the colour beloved by this group as they formulated the ideas that would culminate in the 1911 exhibition that launched the German avant-garde Der Blaue Reiter (The Blue Rider) movement to horrified intakes of breath at the perceived crudity of line and colour. Critics suggest that the many still lifes in interiors Münter did at this period may have resulted from the fact that as the companion of a married man, she found it easier to turn indoors for her subject matter, but this

is an unconvincing argument. In the long Murnau summers, away from the big-city atmosphere of Munich, the four artists created their own world in which art was their ruler. Münter's companions often appeared in her paintings, which included landscapes as well as interiors, and it seems just as likely that she chose to paint interiors rather than having them forced on her by her position as a social outcast. Indeed, by this time, modern artists felt that a painting's technique was just as, if not more, important than its subject. However, I think it is significant that, perhaps because of the unconventional nature of her relationship with Kandinsky, she did not exhibit this work publicly.

The unpeopled interior was an inspiration for the Danish artist Vilhelm Hammershøi who returned to the subject continually through his career. Although, unlike many successful painters of the interior, he does not seem to be speaking about himself or his artistic creed, like them he had to love the space he pictured. He had several homes throughout his life, but he was not inspired to paint them all.

Gabriele Münter
Bedroom in Murnau, 1909

Paintings of the artist's private life start to appear at the end of the nineteenth century. Münter's partner, the artist Kandinsky, can be glimpsed in bed through the door on the left in her house in Murnau.

Opposite: **James Ensor**
My Favourite Room, 1892

A painting that displays the artist's beliefs is a variation on the uninhabited room genre. Ensor's unsettling paintings, set in a conventional bourgeois Belgian interior, act as the artist's manifesto and reveal his distress at contemporary society and his feelings of being unappreciated.

Christianshavn, the old part of Copenhagen where his two favourite homes were located, was close in feel to Amsterdam and both had something about them of the Dutch seventeenth-century interiors he admired.

Dust Motes Dancing in Sunlight (see p.9), which he painted in 1900, is an image of powerful stillness that conjures thoughts of what happens when rooms are left to themselves. It is one of the rare interiors that trap the spirit of the empty room rather than the spirit of those who normally inhabit it. The dust motes and the pattern of the panes inhabit this space, and their magic dance can be interrupted only if the door is opened. It is a painting akin to poetry. Hammershøi worked over his themes obsessively, producing an almost identical painting six years later but without the rays of light, just their patterns on the floor.

In *Open Doors* (1905), Hammershøi introduced an unusual and one of the earliest, if not the earliest, note of unease into a domestic interior. All the doors are open, which gives a sense of instability to the image. The work is about a passage with no conclusion, out of the door on the right, out to the window in the background. There is no furniture, odd for a domestic interior, and the only clues to the status of the owner of this space are the brass doorplates, the handsome proportions of the rooms and the polished wooden floors.

Room portraits were the speciality of the American Walter Gay, who after a conventional artistic education left Boston in 1876 to study for three years with the portraitist Léon Bonnat in Paris. His first paintings, works of history and genre, were well received and two of them were bought by the French government for the national collection. Gay and his wealthy American wife set up home in France and he began to paint the interiors that made his name. Part of a circle of rich and cultured French, English and Americans, including John Singer Sargent, Edith Wharton and Henry James, Gay's market was assured. He was a fortunate man. Far more than an artist who had found a 'line', he was an artist whose line was his pleasure. The paintings he did of his own house outside Paris reveal his susceptibility to the charms of rooms and the importance he attached to surroundings. The colour and light of his paintings, combined with the delicate touch of his fresh, expressive hand, make his paintings as appealing as the interiors they depict.

The personal element means that all the unpeopled interiors in this chapter are autobiography to some degree, from Hammershøi's reticent portraits of the rooms in which he lived to Münter's view into the bedroom she shared with Kandinsky. The paintings of Walter Gay, however, are biography. This is what makes him the true successor of the watercolourists of the interior with which this chapter began. They also show how far the unpeopled interior had travelled in a hundred years. For unlike the watercolours of the early 1800s, Gay's Impressionistic oils of the early 1900s, with their assured brush strokes and pretty colouring, could happily find a place on gallery walls. They represent the acceptance of the domestic interior as a subject by the world of art.

Opposite: **Vilhelm Hammershøi**
Open Doors, 1905

Hammershøi's disconcertingly empty interior, with its open doors, introduces a feeling of unease into paintings of the domestic interior that is not seen again until the Surrealists.

Walter Gay
The Salon, Bréau

Gay made a career of painting room-portraits for his wealthy and cultured clients, but here he paints the château where he lived from 1905 until his death in 1937. His pictures are Impressionistic oil versions of the watercolour rooms with which the nineteenth century opened.

5 seeing the light

The Metropolitan Museum of Art in New York owns a large and striking painting, which may be a self-portrait, of a woman seated by a window drawing, done in 1801 by Marie-Denise Villers. The bare room she sits in offers little in the way of detail. And yet its atmosphere is so powerful that it strikes the viewer as strongly as the young woman hard at work. Villers's decision to underline the seriousness of the artist's attitude to her work by contrasting the sobriety of the cool grey interior light with the bright white exterior light carries more weight than the more conventional contrast of the dedicated artist with the dallying couple outside her window. If Villers had painted the woman traditionally spotlit by the light from the window, the painting would still attract attention for its size and unusual subject. But it is her use of light to construct the woman as serious and the room as silent that makes this such a memorable image.

This use of light to create a mood that parallels the young artist's state of mind is a brilliant development of the group of themes and traditions connected with light, reflections and atmosphere that for centuries had betrayed the hand of the painter sensitive to the magic of light in an interior. The view out of a window; a girl sewing by candlelight; a woman at a mirror; light coming in through a window; the view through a door. With one or two exceptions, none of them were subjects in their own right, since they were not about anything much and anyway tended to be part of a bigger picture. And even the exceptions are hedged around with 'yes buts' and ' not quites'. The older man in the seventeenth-century Dutch

artist Judith Leyster's apparently innocent image of a girl sewing by lamplight, may, in the moralizing fashion of Dutch art, be a procurer trying to tempt Ms Virtue into vice. The woman at a mirror is rarely as simple as she seems. Allegorized and dignified as Vanity, she represents a traditional subject that qualifies as history painting.

Although these themes and traditions are the ancestors of the paintings in this chapter, the works here are different. Thanks to the spread of the more modest tastes of the picture-buying middle classes and the weakening grip of history painting, the new nineteenth-century breed of artists was able to develop these corners and glimpses of windows, mirrors, light and lamps into atmospheric interiors that are finished images in themselves.

The work of one such artist appeared early in the nineteenth century. The fame of German-born and Copenhagen-trained Georg Friedrich Kersting, whose career included painting portraits and supervising the Meissen manufactory, today rests on the paintings of everyday life that display his fascination with light effects in rooms. They are the sort of works that have traditionally been categorized as genre, but unlike genre painting, there is no moral and no attempt to tell a story. Indeed, Kersting consciously baffles our attempts to read too much into the works by painting people from the back, the side or in shadow, forcing the viewer to peer closely to make out the facial details that the artist clearly feels are irrelevant to his purpose.

Instead of inviting us to deduce a story, he aims to give us the sense of what it feels like to be in the room he puts

Marie-Denise Villers

Young Woman Drawing, 1801

Villers contrasts the sombre interior
with the golden day outside to suggest
the young artist's dedication to her
work. This use of light to suggest
a state of mind is a development
of earlier depictions of rooms which
betrayed the hands of painters sensitive
to the magic of light in an interior.

before us. Kersting gives us no chance to engage with the subject of *Girl Embroidering* of 1814 in any conventional way: at first we do not see her face and when we finally notice it reflected in the mirror he denies us the opportunity to meet her eyes. In fact, despite the title, I do not think that the woman and her work are the subject at all: it is the light in the room. What the painter does is place us in the room. We stand to the side of the woman and observe her at work in the light from the window. And as we stand there, we take in the beauties of the room as Kersting perceived them.

Louise Seidler, the model for this painting, was an artist. Twenty-eight at the time, she had, unusually for a woman, taken classes at the Dresden Academy and three years earlier had painted a portrait of Goethe, one of the many intellectuals she mixed with until her death in 1866. But none of this is alluded to here. Seidler is merely the peg on which Kersting hangs his real interest, which is to convey his awareness of light's role in making things visible when it enters a room. This observation may seem self-evident, but we have only to look at other interiors to understand the special vision Kersting possessed as he recreates the grades of light as it loses power in its journey from the window. From this image alone, I would argue that Kersting believed that light was an active force, a force that could create. He chose the interior as his laboratory, the place where he could examine light's ability to generate its own special effects.

While Kersting's interest in light could be argued to have a scientific basis, in the sense of careful observation, the goal of the German romantic painter Caspar David Friedrich was to use light in the service of spirituality. All of Friedrich's art is a personal exploration of the divine in daily life, taking nature, for example, through a series of gradations from foreground green grass to mid-ground brown hills to background pale mountain, or creating parallels between the spiky upturned branches of a fir tree and the pinnacles of a Gothic church. In 1822, in his search for ways to express his view of the connection between earth and heaven, Friedrich turned indoors and painted one of his most influential works: *Woman at a Window*. This new pictorial theme, in which the interior

Opposite: **Judith Leyster**
Man Offering Money to a Young Woman, 1631

In the fashion typical of seventeenth-century Dutch interiors, the surface peace of the subject hides a deeper moral meaning. The serene seamstress is apparently oblivious to the coins held in the hand of the fur-hatted seducer.

Georg Friedrich Kersting

Girl Embroidering, 1814

Despite the title, the window is the point of this painting. The girl, the artist Louise Seidler, is merely the means for Kersting to chronicle the changes in light as it enters the room. With his lack of interest in telling a story and his fascination with light effects, Kersting was a pioneer in making the domestic interior a subject in its own right.

Friedrich's art can be seen as an attempt
to unite the earthly and spiritual worlds.
Here, in a new development of the
interior, he paints his wife with her
feet firmly in the room while her head
is in another world beyond, suggested
by the cross of the window bars.

plays an intrinsic part, of the woman seen from the back as
she looks out of a window, was an inspired way to suggest
the human need to link into the spiritual that lies behind
reality. The interior from which Friedrich's wife Caroline
Bonner watches the river Elbe is the earthly home of the
contemplative woman who looks out into the world beyond –
it is not chance that the bars of the window form a cross.
The juxtaposition of the dark interior, the woman's
habitat, with the pale trees and mast-filled square of the
world outside, and the woman's back as she turns from
the security of the interior to the unknowable exterior
creates a mood of human yearning. It is brilliant for another
reason, too: the figure is a surrogate for ourselves, mirroring
our position as we look at the painting, inviting us to step
into her shoes.

At some point around mid-century, the spiritual and
scientific interests in light, which had inspired Friedrich and
Kersting in their different ways, dropped away to leave light
in an interior as an acceptable subject in its own right. We
can see this happening in the way Friedrich's image of the
woman gazing out of the window becomes a new subject
that could be copied, argued with and imagined differently
in the following decades of the nineteenth century. It was
particularly resonant for German and Scandinavian painters
right up until the early twentieth century, though few shared
Friedrich's particular spiritual cast of mind. Moritz von
Schwind's *Morning* (1860) is a down-to-earth interpretation.
Less a spiritual exercise than an expression of delight in a
new day, the details of the interior are used to make the
point that the woman has paused in her familiar morning
ritual to look at the world outside her window, a point that in
earlier centuries would not have been considered worthy of a

Moritz von Schwind
Morning, 1860

Schwind ignores the spiritual element
of Friedrich's image of the woman at the
window to create a mood of domestic
comfort and delight in a new day.

Vilhelm Hammershøi
Bedroom, 1890

Hammershøi's homage to Friedrich shows his wife looking down from the bedroom window but unlike his predecessor the mystery comes from the atmosphere of the room itself and not the spirituality symbolized by the world outside.

Right: **Berthe Morisot**
The Artist's Sister at a Window, 1869

Morisot's window paintings emphasize the female element of the domestic interior with their subjects who ignore the world outside their walls. Feminist theory suggests that the woman at the window is a metaphor for her confined position in nineteenth-century society.

Opposite: **Berthe Morisot**
Daydreaming, 1877

The impact of this image of a cloistered bourgeois woman encased in comfortable domesticity comes from the gauzy curtains that veil her from the world outside.

painting to itself. In 1890, the young Hammershøi painted his new wife Ida looking out of the window of their home in Strandgade. It is a homage to Friedrich but without his desire to represent the interior as a launching pad for the spiritual world beyond; Hammershøi's room is the subject of his painting and the woman a device to anchor us in it.

I see the woman at a window as a variation on the theme of the interior, since in every case the window to the exterior is there to suggest its domestic opposite. Feminist theory has suggested that the nineteenth-century theme of the woman at a window underlines her position in society, a position akin to a caged bird, a tempting explanation in the light of our knowledge of the restricted lives of many women of the middle classes. A work that supports this theory is the Impressionist Berthe Morisot's painting of 1869, *The Artist's Sister at a Window*, which shows her seated and studying a fan in front of an open window. Morisot had a lifelong habit of basing her work on her family, so she

probably chose her sister because she was an available model, the room in her house because it was a private and convenient place to work, and the pose because it was a simple one for her sister to hold. But all the common sense in the world cannot take away from the resulting image of female passivity. She does not look out. She sits quietly. It is as if the exterior world is not hers to enter.

Eight years later, in 1877, Morisot painted *Daydreaming*, a young woman with her feet on the sofa and her back to a window whose light is veiled in filmy fabric. Of course, Berthe Morisot, Impressionist, is aware of the repoussoir effects beloved of Edgar Degas, of course she is aware of her brother-in-law Manet's portraits of women stretched out on sofas, of course she is challenged by the task of finding painted equivalents for the light that pours through the window and touches the dress in zigzags of pale paint. And yet, for a woman to paint another woman with her back to a window has overtones of special knowledge, of the bourgeois woman's time to dream in a private interior, made

even more private by the way the outside world is curtained off behind her.

By the second half of the century, the woman at the window had become an important theme in art, a pairing as acceptable as mother and child. But despite its special relationship with women, the window is not reserved for them. Thirty years before Friedrich's *Woman at a Window*, J.H.W. Tischbein painted a dashing portrait of Goethe at the window of his room in Rome. It may have to do with our feelings about rooms as women's natural habitat, but there is something about this work which, in giving full rein to the romantic element of his dress and pose, seems to make him less a prisoner of the interior than a man surveying a world that could be his whenever he wishes. It is a painting of a pause before the plunge, in comparison to Friedrich's woman in her soft slippers who can only watch the ships, not sail away on them.

The Impressionist Gustave Caillebotte painted men as well as women at the window. Caillebotte is a painter whose feet are firmly on the Paris pavement and in its devotion to the here and now, his art is totally of its time. He was a friend of the Impressionists, a talented amateur and a collector, and he had clearly absorbed the message of their supporter, the novelist and critic Edmond Duranty, who argued for subject matter taken from everyday life: 'From indoors we communicate with the outside world through windows. A window is yet another frame that is continually with us during the time we spend at home, and that time is considerable. Depending on whether we are near or far, seated or standing, the window frames the scene outside in the most unexpected and changeable ways.'[1] This thought, which could not be further from Friedrich's vision of the window leading to the afterlife, is echoed by many of Caillebotte's window paintings, which conjure up bourgeois respectability rather than anything more elevated.

Caillebotte keeps close to the masculine stereotype. There is little wistfulness about his images of men reading in the light of a window or surveying the world from one. The solidity of his subjects and their surroundings, all red velvet and bourgeois comfort, forbid this. *Young Man at his Window* of 1875, a back view of his brother René who has risen from

Opposite: **J.H.W. Tischbein**

Goethe at the Window of his Apartment by the Corso in Rome, 1787

The images of men at windows are different from those of women. In Rome in the eighteenth century the writer and intellectual Goethe surveys a world that could be his whenever he wished.

Gustave Caillebotte

Young Man at his Window, 1875

Caillebotte paints his brother as both lord of the interior (the comfortable red chair in which he has been sitting) and of the exterior (the Paris street he stands to survey) in a telling image of man's place in modern life.

Gustave Caillebotte
Interior, 1880

A handful of late nineteenth-century paintings depict the intimacy and comfort – and perhaps the boredom – of middle-class married life by contrasting it with the public world outside the window.

his chair better to see the activity of the street, displays idle curiosity as much as anything else. Like Goethe before him, Caillebotte's figure stands in an easy but powerful manner with his hands in his pockets, surveying the scene which is as much his as the comfortably furnished interior. Without necessarily being conscious of it, the viewer understands the code. The interior is his, but so is the exterior. He is appraising, but he is not longing.

Caillebotte's women on the other hand are a little more surprising. They are less active, it is true, and they do not stand as if they own the view. But neither do they yearn. Caillebotte's vision of women is more down-to-earth than the theory would have it. Far from the exterior representing a world of excitement that is barred to them, his women look sturdy enough to take public transport or visit the new department stores.

In 1880, Caillebotte painted *Interior*, in which a couple evoke the settled state of marriage. The seated man looks at his paper not at his wife; she looks out of her window into an identical window opposite, which also frames a woman looking out. Ten years later, Paul Signac produced his version of this subject, *A Paris Sunday* (1890), in which he gives equal importance to the woman at the window, the

Paul Signac
A Paris Sunday, 1890

Signac's avant-garde technique, derived from the colour theories and form of Seurat's pointillism, turns the furnishings of this conventional bourgeois interior into a striking image of colour, pattern and shapes that leap with a life of their own.

man tending to the fire and the carefully furnished and carpeted interior. More than seventy years earlier, in 1817, Kersting had painted a couple conversing amicably by the window of an uncarpeted living room, the woman dressed to go out with a basket on her arm and a bonnet on her head. The depiction of intimacy without a sexual element is typical of several nineteenth-century images of couples in interiors. In the case of Kersting, they are conversing without a hint of flirtation. In the case of Caillebotte and Signac, the man and woman are separately absorbed, the woman looking out, the man involved in reading or seeing to the fire. Perhaps the sexless atmosphere is connected to the daylight and the window.

The view through a window, the strategy invented by the Netherlandish artists of the fifteenth century to counteract the claustrophobia of their tiny images, and open doors, the compositional device developed by the seventeenth-century Dutch to create recession and visual interest through views into other rooms, also take on a life of their own in the nineteenth century, becoming the reason for a painting rather than a pictorial device within it.

Traditionally, the view through a window or a door served a variety of purposes. It could anchor a painting in reality, which is what Campin's follower does in *c.*1440 when he paints a ladder against a house in a northern town outside the Virgin Mary's window (see p.29). It could advance a story. In the first painting of *Marriage à la Mode*, Hogarth shows a stately home outside the window in the process of being rebuilt as a way of explaining why the elderly aristocrat is selling his son to the daughter of a wealthy city merchant – her dowry will complete the building works.

In the nineteenth century, such meanings faded away alongside the desire for narrative, and the view through the door or window was often used simply on the principle of contrast, the world beyond the room stressing the quality of the interior. Monet's unusual view of his wife Camille seen through a window in the snow in about 1873 relies on the juxtaposition of interior warmth with external cold for its success. Pretty hints of greenery glimpsed through open doors were much used at the end of the nineteenth century to create interiors suffused with light and freshness.

Opposite: **Georg Friedrich Kersting**
Couple at the Window, 1817

Kersting depicts a quiet moemnt in a
room whose details are shown in the
mirror on the right.

Claude Monet
*The Red Kerchief: Portrait of Camille, c.*1873

Monet did several paintings of his
wife Camille and young son Jean at
this period. Without the contrast
supplied by the foreground room,
the wonderful image of Camille in
the snow would lose its impact.

Stanhope Forbes
The Harbour Window, 1910

Forbes attempts the difficult task of balancing exterior and interior in this painting made in Newlyn, the Cornish artists' colony in which he was a major figure.

Sometimes artists go further and try and capture the view through the window as a kind of trophy for the interior. It is not every artist who can keep the spectator inside the room when the outside beckons. When the English artist Stanhope Forbes paints the exterior view in *The Harbour Window* (1910) we go straight into it. Even though he has supplied us with a woman sewing in a charming interior, it is not enough to hold us back. Given the fact that he paints the jostling boats in a higher colour key, which draws the spectator beyond the room, maybe that was his intention. Raoul Dufy on the other hand manages to keep the spectator indoors. By using the same tonality for interior and exterior in *Open Window, Nice* (1928), he manages to capture the view as one of the pleasures of the blue and orange room.

Despite the many windows in the work of Vilhelm Hammershøi, he never paints the view outside them. Reversing the tradition first seen with the fifteenth-century Netherlandish artists, he does not offer us a window to see out of but to bring things in to us. It is the light coming into a room that is his subject, not the view beyond the room. He is fascinated by the way a window throws lozenges of light on a wall, lays a pattern at our feet on the floor, or offers a contrast to the grey walls around it with its pale rectangles of light. If he includes a woman in his later interiors, he paints her from the back in the same geometric way as his sparse pieces of furniture, and as we stand facing in the same direction as she does, she is our eyes into the depths of the image. In these paintings, in which the woman's gaze is into the room, not out of it, he uses her in the same way he uses windows, to emphasize the interior not lead you out of it.

Another theme that makes the nineteenth-century journey into a subject in its own right is the woman at the mirror. As one of the great voyeuristic subjects, it has fascinated male painters. In contrast to the power of the window to take the woman out of herself, the mirror throws her back on herself and for centuries a woman holding up a mirror was the recognized manner of painting the sin of vanity. From Tintoretto to Rubens, all the great figure painters produced a version. It was not until the end of the eighteenth century that the woman at the mirror lost these classical associations and became a way to suggest female private life. The woman alone with herself, private, preparing herself for her public, interested the influential painter of Denmark's 'golden age', C.W. Eckersberg, in his later years, and in 1866 the Italian Cletofonte Preti painted a beauty pinning her hair before the mirror in *La Toilette*. References to the room, even if it is no more than a chair, a chest or a table, are always included as part of the woman's private world. It matters to the sense of these works that the interior is included, for it locates the women in a recognizably domestic setting rather than the sensuous fabric-filled interior of a Vanity.

In 1827, Kersting painted *In Front of the Mirror*, a work that deserves to be pulled out of the genre category where it is normally located. Here the mirror is just what it seems – a device to show us the woman readying her hair to receive the huge hat whose yellow sings out loudly in the light from the window. This is a fine example of the new domestic interior in its lack of narrative and its determination to catch the daytime light effects surrounding the woman preparing to go out.

As with the window, the woman at a mirror appears more often after 1850 as the movement to put daily life in art becomes more important, particularly among the Impressionists. Berthe Morisot produced several works on this theme in the 1870s. In *Psyche* (1876), the French name for a type of long looking glass, her model surveys herself from the side. This painting is often compared with the rather bold charm of *Nana* (1877) done by Manet, but this seems unfair to both of them. Manet's painting, which is thought to have been inspired by the novel about a courtesan by his friend and supporter Emile Zola, a claim confirmed by the top-hatted man sitting to her right, is practically a narrative work. Nana looks at the viewer, engaging with him – it can only be a him considering her state of partial undress – and she is applying lipstick, a far more brazen activity than Morisot's model's sidelong survey.

Morisot's painting is very different in its attempt to paint a private moment in a woman's relationship with a mirror, a relationship she knew and could paint with conviction. She did a number of mirror subjects at this time: *Lady at her Toilet*

Georg Friedrich Kersting
In Front of the Mirror, 1827

As everyday life became more important as a subject in the nineteenth century, a woman at a mirror and the light streaming into a room was accepted as sufficient basis for a painting.

Berthe Morisot
Psyche, 1876

Morisot's painting exemplifies the mirror's artistic journey from Renaissance emblem of vanity to familiar domestic object. The feminity of this Parisian bedroom envelops the young woman as she appraises herself in the full-length mirror.

Edouard Manet

Nana, 1877

Everything about this painting, including the man on the right, indicates that this woman is used to receiving visitors in her room – a more public than private space.

Berthe Morisot
Young Woman Powdering her Face, 1877

Morisot was a sensitive painter of women at their private tasks. Here, the sitter is alone with her image in a pretty bedroom, readying herself for the evening ahead.

(*c*.1875) and *Young Woman Powdering her Face* (1877) are beautiful examples of this theme, the light and reflections created by her gauzy web of brushstrokes suggesting the purity of this private female world. Instead of being painted as the objects of male curiosity, these are insider paintings of women absorbed in powdering, checking and tucking in loose strands of hair. In all of them, the fittings of the rooms, the looking glass, the pretty fabrics and the upholstered chairs signal a contemporary female interior space that would be recognizable to the viewer.

In 1865–70, while still an adolescent, Eva Gonzalès painted *La Psyche*, a young woman staring at herself in a full-length mirror, for which the artist's sister Jeanne was the model. This early work, painted in the conservative technique she favoured before she went to Manet for instruction, is a private view of a young woman appraising herself, her proper bourgeois nature emphasized by the uprights of the mirror and the horizontals of the furniture. Only a few years later, *Le Petit Lever* (*c*.1875–6), a painting of a young woman having her hair dressed, shows evidence of a change of vision on the artist's part. Now under the influence of Impressionism and, it seems, the eighteenth century, Gonzalès shows the young woman and her maid in a more ornate setting, with the rococo flourishes of a curving mirror, a prettily shaped dressing table and the hangings of a bed creating a far more worldly effect than the work of the previous decade.

Occasionally, artists use the mirror to expand the space in an image. An anonymous Russian artist in the second quarter of the century pictures two women chatting and sewing in what the viewer gradually realizes is a mirror. In 1894, Roger Fry used a mirror as the background to his portrait of the socialist Edward Carpenter, thereby expanding the room he stands in to create a huge interior space.

The oil lamps which were an increasingly common replacement for candles from the end of the eighteenth century were a milestone on the road to domestic comfort, for their stronger light extended activities such as sewing, drawing and playing cards into the evening. They also opened the eyes of artists to the exciting new lighting effects which were now part of the evening ambiance of the home. Shadows and glimpses of light in dark were the traditional tools for creating a mood of horror or mystery in narrative works, but the new kinds of artificial light revealed the mystery and beauty that now could be found in the home. One thing stayed the same, however. Traditionally, the more dramatic light effects had been reserved for men whereas

Anon
Reflection in a Mirror, c.1825–50

This intriguing Russian painting
explores the pictorial possibilities
of mirrors in a domestic interior.
The reflections and counter reflections
supply the spectator with the depth
and distance more commonly
associated with landscape.

Georg Friedrich Kersting
Man Reading by Lamplight, 1814

Oil lamps, which replaced candles at the
end of the eighteenth century, opened
artists' eyes to the exciting new effects
of artificial light offered by the home.
The strange shadows are as important
a subject as the man reading and are an
early example of the purely visual as a
subject for art.

artistic decorum decreed that illuminated effects centred on women were more domestic in feeling. A rare exception to this rule are the macabre witches' gatherings of the Neapolitan painter Salvator Rosa, but then witches did not conform to accepted ideas of femininity. This gender difference continues into the nineteenth century. Whereas paintings of women by lamplight concentrate on the effect of a little light in a dark space, men by lamplight are often an excuse for an exploration of strange and showy light effects. In 1814, Kersting delights in noting the huge and oddly shaped shadows made by the lamp on the wall behind the subject of *Man Reading by Lamplight*.

Like Kersting, the Danish artist Wilhelm Bendz was fascinated by the world around him. In *A Smoking Party*, painted in 1827–8 when he was twenty-four and only four years before his death, Bendz shows his fascination with the way lamplight can make a familiar room strange by depicting the weirdly elongated shadows it casts on the walls. The Argand lamp that illuminates the room was an oil-lamp refinement of 1784; it reduced flickering and strengthened the quality of the light.

Wilhelm Bendz

A Smoking Party, 1827–8

The night-time light effects of oil lamps, which extended activities into the evening, and the development of the home as a centre for recreation, were two of the elements that made the domestic interior a new object of interest for artists in the early years of the nineteenth century.

Adolph Menzel

Living Room with the Artist's Sister, 1847

Menzel's group of small interiors painted around mid-century show his fascination with light in an interior, although their medium, card, reveals his reluctance to see them as works for exhibition. In the second half of the century, such impressions of light in the home became a sufficient subject for finished works.

Robert Braithwaite Martineau
The Last Chapter, 1863

Martineau's reader is surrounded by
the comfort and paraphernalia of a
Victorian home as she kneels to catch
the firelight on the last pages of her
novel. Books are frequent accessories,
like gloves or small dogs, in paintings
of women, but this image, echoing
Liotard's portrait of Marie-Adelaide
of France over a hundred years earlier,
celebrates the active pleasure of reading.

Adolph Menzel was another artist intrigued by artificial
light in interiors: 'On one occasion, his sister, who had
called us to a table more than once, founded [*sic*] herself in
a spot where the lighting was unusually interesting. This
provided the opportunity for a study which took some time,'
wrote a friend.[2] *Living Room with the Artist's Sister* (1847) is
an example of this type of family night-time scene, and
while this particular painting may have only been a sketch,
the woman by lamplight, like the other vignettes of this
chapter, would become an accepted subject later in
the century.

If more proof is needed that by the second half of the
century the home had become a subject for art, it is offered
by the paintings that centre on firelight. The hearth, after
all, is a metonym for the home. In *The Last Chapter* (1863), the
English artist Robert Braithwaite Martineau, an associate
of the Pre-Raphaelites, painted a young woman kneeling
by the fire in a darkened night-time room comfortably
furnished with paintings and a piano. The artist shows her
in thrall to a novel as she holds up her book to catch the
glow from the firelight on its pages. A warm fire, a naked
back and a homely room are the reasons for Vallotton's

Félix Vallotton
Nude at the Stove, 1900

Among a number of interior images Vallotton made around 1900, this stands out for its strong shapes and for capturing the warmth and importance of the stove in the days before central heating.

Nude at the Stove of 1900. No moral is implied, no title supplied to arouse our interest, no classical link is suggested to raise the tone. All that is necessary to qualify this as an acceptable image is a back view of a naked woman warming herself by the fire. The nineteenth century has succeeded in turning the little themes and corners of paintings into stand-alone subjects. Finally, two centuries after the other genres developed out of the background, the interior does it too.

Carl Holsøe
The Artist's Home at Lyngby

By the end of the nineteenth century, the domestic interior was a subject in its own right. Danish artists such as Holsøe were masters at controlling colour and light to evoke the pleasurable atmosphere of the home.

6 the portrait interior

The conventional view that daily life and portraiture did not mix had a long, strong life. There is a passage in James Northcote's recollections, where he remembers his days as an apprentice in the studio of Sir Joshua Reynolds in the 1770s, that shows his unquestioning acceptance of the casual approach of his day to the sitter's surroundings: 'I should have painted in a red curtain, but the damask is lost which the curtain used to be painted from. I shall make part of a building appear behind the curtains and a landscape in the background.'[1] The kind of thinking that would see the appeal of painting sitters in their own interiors was hardly to be expected and certainly not encouraged in the studio of a man who, wearing his hat as president of the Royal Academy, told his students that: 'He therefore who in his practice of portrait-painting wishes to dignify his subject, which we will suppose to be a lady, will not paint her in the modern dress, the familiarity of which alone is sufficient to destroy all dignity.'[2] This thinking went on into the twentieth century. Perhaps not Reynolds's plea for classical dress, but certainly the feeling that realism should be avoided. 'Reality in backgrounds is fatal,' thundered the Royal Academician Sir Hubert von Herkomer, portrait painter of the mostly male civic worthies at the turn of the twentieth century. 'Everything must give way to the face of the sitter…I go so far as to say the more elaborate a background, the less a portrait!'[3]

This thinking is still found up to the present day. In his 1971 book on portrait painting, the American portraitist Everett Raymond Kinstler began his chapter on backgrounds with the words: 'Backgrounds should be nothing more than the word implies; they should stay back! A scenic designer once told me that if a set is repeatedly applauded by the audience, the designer is doing a disservice to the playwright and creating a background is like laying the scene for a play.' And he ended the chapter with the words: 'I think by now I have emphasized enough the importance of anything that conflicts with the portrait of the man. If the detail takes on too much importance, reduce its impact or eliminate it!'[4] Painting my self-portrait in an evening class, I was told that the way to think about the background was as a negative space, the kind of advice that has become standard in a post-modern world that thinks of canvases in two-dimensional terms.

However, not everyone subscribed to the view, seen at its most extreme in Reynolds's recommendation of vaguely classical costumes, that everyday life and portraiture did not mix. The eighteenth century produced a number of exceptions who gave the interior an essential role in their portraits, as we saw when Devis was picturing the country gentry in their imaginary living rooms and Zoffany in their real ones. This new trend gathered strength in the nineteenth century. Where once the background had been something that should not offer distracting competition, some artists now saw it as a positive addition to their depiction of the sitter.

Despite the strictures against too much going on in portraits, which all painters knew, some of the best interiors are to be found in the portraits produced in the years 1820–50, when a fashion was born for what could be called the portrait interior in the countries that shared the

English School
Group Portrait of Three Men,
early 19th century

Despite the portraiture convention
that surroundings should be
subordinate to subject, this
unknown artist believes the sitters'
setting is as important as their faces.

Wilhelm Bendz

Interior in the Amaliegade, 1830

After two decades of war, the Germans, Danes and Austrians turned inwards and found pleasure in their homes and friends and families. One of the artist's brothers stands at a desk while the other sits to read in this most domesticated of student lodgings.

Biedermeier culture of comfortable domesticity. The name Biedermeier was invented by two German writers to express the personality behind their gently satirical poems and short stories about the middle classes of the 1840s and 1850s. The name (*Meier* is a common German surname and *bieder* means domestic) was adopted and backdated at the century's end as the term for this central European culture whose visual aspect is familiar to us through paintings.

From the traditionalists' point of view, the Biedermeier portrait interior is an artistic hybrid, a blurring of the lines between genres. To me, it is a clever artistic invention to cope with the social developments of the day, a creative blending of genre painting with the portrait format in order to express the values of the bourgeois way of life, whose practitioners wanted portraits of their much-loved homes instead of the nonspecific curtains and pillars of conventional portraiture.

The portrait interior was aided by the fact that art was changing. The eighteenth-century belief in idealizing and generalizing, which in portrait practice meant a smoothing out of flaws and idiosyncracies and a downplaying of the background, was being replaced by an interest in exact reporting. The interest in realism is one of the most important strands of nineteenth-century art. At the start of the century, it was preparing itself for a long run in which it would take a number of forms that had as their goal the convincing reproduction of the world around us: realism, Pre-Raphaelitism, naturalism, Impressionism. Difficult to define, it could be all things to all artists. In the name of realism, the historical painter Paul Delaroche could painstakingly reproduce every muscle of his models and every crease of their clothes in order to convince the spectator of the reality of his historical scenes, while also in the name of realism Gustave Courbet could depict the unidealized nudes and rural society of his day. The unstoppable march of realism, in all its variations, provided the perfect style to celebrate the new importance of domestic life. Realism had always been the favoured style for genre painting, for the obvious reason that to idealize a scene of everyday life would undermine the desired realistic effect. Now genre was joining forces with a newly realistic portraiture.

This central European flowering of painted domesticity is conventionally traced back to the Congress of Vienna of 1815, which marked the end of almost two decades of war. In Vienna, Dresden, Berlin and Copenhagen, the middle and upper classes greeted the peace by turning their backs on public life and making their homes the centre of their world. Fulfilment for men as well as women was found in the home, thereby creating a new subject for representation in art. 'The living room, the focal point of the family, was accorded such a degree of significance and importance that it now became an independent theme in painting,' wrote Christian Witt-Dörring in 1979.[5]

It is interesting to speculate why painting families in their interiors should have seemed so congenial to the Biedermeier portrait painters. The official advice on painting portraits had not changed, so other factors must

have had a hand in it. The watercolour room-portrait probably encouraged the use of naturalistic settings, and the new bourgeois-inspired informality adopted by some of the rich and royal in their portraits probably filtered back to the middle classes as a style enhanced by its grand associations. In addition, as homes became more appealing to both sexes as the centre of family life, new ways of thinking about the interior developed. People began to see their interiors as reflections of themselves, controlling what went into them. But I suspect the clinching fact in elevating the status of the home is that the men of the middle and upper classes began to play a greater part in domestic life. As husbands and fathers as well as painters, the artists found ways to incorporate the newly important home into their portraits of the patrons whose values they shared.

Biedermeier portraiture offered the domestic interior an important route into art. The importance of the home and family life in the German states, and to a degree the countries around them, made it natural for artists to show their sitters in their surroundings at this period. From the point of view of today's viewer, these enchanting images do not just convey the sitter's pride in family, which has always been one of the goals of portraiture, they also suggest the values of their bourgeois way of life, the status and character of the sitters, and the pleasure of living in this manner. Supported by their realistic presentation, Biedermeier interiors still fascinate us. It is the 'this is how it was' quality of *Interior in the Amaliegade*, a painting that the Danish artist Wilhelm Bendz made in 1830 of his two brothers in their student lodgings, which makes it so full of interest for the viewer, from the stand-up desk to the painted walls and bare wood floor of the light and airy room.

This naturalistic treatment makes an instructive contrast with Devis's works of a century earlier, for despite Devis's picture of an ideal Georgian furnishing layout, it is not easy to imagine any of his sitters living an enjoyable life in these chilly expanses. Even when he supplies the children of the family with flutes or a house of cards, it is hard to imagine them actually picking them up or playing with them. By contrast, the polished floors, comfortable sofas and medium-sized rooms of the Biedermeier paintings

Friedrich von Amerling
Rudolf von Arthaber with his Children, 1837

The Biedermeier artists created a blend of genre painting and portraiture to convey the period's pleasure in the home. Respect for children is expressed through the objects strewn informally on the chair and the relaxed poses of the sitters.

Emilius Ditlev Baerentzen
Winther Family, 1827

When domestic life becomes important, so do domestic details. The refreshments on the table, the visitors, the curtains, shutters and polished furniture, the family portraits on the wall, express an air of respectable comfortable domesticity.

seem to encourage informal contact between the members of the depicted families, allowing us a glimpse of how their lives were lived. There are books, flowers, pets, toys and musical instruments: we can almost hear the sounds and we can surmise that the children are allowed to jump on the sofa and run around. Though the device chosen by the Austrian artist Friedrich von Amerling for his portrait of the widower *Rudolf von Arthaber with his Children* (1837) is conventional and a little sad, for he shows the textile manufacturer looking at a painting of his dead wife, the overall impression of the work is of the coziness of family life and the energy of children. The fabrics everywhere suggest warmth and comfort, and the toys on the floor and sofa add an appealing untidiness.

The portrait of the *Winther Family* (1827) by the Austrian artist Emilius Ditlev Baerentzen glows with the natural light of a sensibly furnished interior that makes no claims to put its sitters above their station. Curtains frame the town where they live out their middle-class existence, the church tower underlines the religious basis of their lives, and the light from the open shutters to the left allows the painter to make a silhouette of the bending woman's profile against her companion's light, bright sleeve. Baerentzen's success is that by creating a convincing illusion of realism – for though one suspects it must be, we cannot be sure that it is a portrait of a real room in a real house – he convinces the spectator of the pleasures of a modest family life. In this he is helped by the inclusion of the ceiling, which adds an extra layer of detail, and by the natural poses of the sitters.

Alexei Venetsianov
Prince V.P. Kochubei in his Study, c.1834

An influential teacher, Venetsianov
was known for his paintings of natural
light in interiors. This work is a marriage
between the watercolour room-portraits
of the start of the century and the
conventional format of aristocratic
portraiture.

The Biedermeier countries were not the only ones where the domestic interior made inroads into portraiture in the first half of the nineteenth century. It happened in Russia, too, though by a different route. With Russia, there is a proven link between the watercolour room-portraits and the entrance of the realistic interior into oil paintings. The groundwork was laid at the end of the previous century when the Imperial Academy of Arts in St Petersburg encouraged students to paint interiors through its courses on perspectival architectural painting and small Dutch and Flemish paintings of the seventeenth century.[6] This trend was strengthened in 1819 when the artist Alexei Venetsianov began spreading his ideas through his influential art school in St Petersburg and through courses he offered peasants on his country estate. More down to earth than the St Petersburg Academy, the Venetsianov school ignored history painting in favour of classes on perspective, landscape and interiors. The original goal seems to have been to train artists to record the rooms of the aristocracy, but before long, encouraged by the growth of the middle classes and their specific taste in art, room interiors became a fruitful subject for oil paintings. Venetsianov himself was known for them. One of his most famous works, *The Morning of a Landowner's Wife* (1823) reveals his sensitivity to the effects of light in a domestic interior while his portrait of *Prince V.P. Kochubei in his Study* (c.1834) combines the Comte de Clarac's informal presentation of Caroline Murat with the respectful quality of the conventional aristocratic portrait that aims to dazzle with its grandeur. Like many watercolour rooms, it is a room-portrait that insists on including details of the ceiling in its portrayal of the prince in his surroundings. It is so precise that the study could be recreated in the event of fire.

Venetsianov was not the only Russian to pay as much attention to the sitters' surroundings as to the sitters themselves. Fyodor Petrovich Tolstoy, an aristocratic neoclassical relief sculptor and medallist who was curator at the Hermitage and vice president of the St Petersburg Academy, is just as interested in his perspective portrait of the enfilade of rooms as he is in the glamorous parents and their modest daughters in his painting *Portrait of a Family*

(1830). In fact, this is a self-portrait: the apartment was indeed full of statues and paintings 'and in the tall, luminous rooms a profound silence prevailed'.[7] One of the particularly appealing things about this painting is that it offers a compendium of the painter's tastes. We tend to think of styles in art as tidy sets of characteristics because that is the way we learn about them, but it is rare in real life to find a room completely given over to one style. The stylistic clues in this interior reveal an unexpected elision of the neoclassical and the romantic: the lyre light fitting, the lifesize casts and the griffon-legged chair are all neoclassical but the artist is as Byronic as Eugene Onegin in Pushkin's poem (1825–31), and the seascape behind him, painted in the manner of Claude-Joseph Vernet (which Tolstoy may have done himself), is equally romantic.

Fyodor Petrovich Tolstoy
Portrait of a Family, 1830

The aristocrat and artist presents himself as the epitome of Byronic elegance in this portrait with his family, set in his glamorous apartment, which is shown full of works of art and with an impressive axial view.

Pushkarev is clearly as interested in the contents of his sitter's home as he was in the sitter himself. A painting like this, from about the mid-nineteenth century, exemplifies the journey of the domestic interior into artistic acceptability.

In the desire to make a two-dimensional canvas into a three-dimensional room, the Russian artists were fonder of the effects of recession than the German artists of the Biedermeier whose interiors tend to be enclosed. Kapiton Zelentsov, who was a follower of Venetsianov, favours the view into far rooms in his painting of two elegant young men and a dog from the 1820s. With the help of the perspective of the floor, Prokofy Yegorovich Pushkarev's *At Home*, from about the mid-nineteenth century, takes us straight into the room at the back of the painting. Quite

different from the Biedermeier convention of cosy little pools of chairs and tables, is the way the furniture is aligned along the walls. It is an example of differing furnishing styles being given different artistic treatments.

The century's interest in realism had one of its periodic flareups in London at mid-century when seven young writers and artists founded the Pre-Raphaelite Brotherhood, an attempt to look behind the generalized, idealized art of Raphael at the detailed imagery and gawky figures of the Italian and Netherlandish artists of the fifteenth century.

Kapiton Zelentsov
Interior, 1820s

Russian domestic arrangements seem far less cozy than their Biedermeier counterparts, which tend to stress enclosure and comfort. The central space and perspective views through open doors are typical of Russian portrait interiors.

John Everett Millais
*James Wyatt and his Granddaughter,
Mary Wyatt*, 1849

The young Pre-Raphaelite painter
is here trying out his artistic beliefs
on a portrait of his patron and his
granddaughter. The insistance on
clarity and detail, which is so typical
of the fifteenth-century portraits
Millais admired, leads to a setting
that unfashionably refuses to stay
subordinate to the sitters.

In 1849, the precocious John Everett Millais, at twenty the youngest of the group, tried out his hyper-realistic style on his commissioned portrait of James Wyatt, an Oxford picture dealer who was one of his earliest patrons. The meticulous reproduction of Wyatt and his granddaughter, he so protective, she so trusting, amid the family china, the plants in the garden and the fabrics that meet the eye in every corner of the room, was everything that conventional portraiture scorned. 'The infinite patience and imitative skill in draughtsmanship, the brilliance of execution, and the power of reproducing the brightness of sunlight, have manifestly been acquired before the lesson had been learned of harmonious effect and of subordinating the parts....It

has all been set down with pitiless and remorseless solitude.'[8] The criticism could have come come straight out of the constantly reprinted *The Art of Portrait Painting in Oil Colours.*

One British group increasingly shown in their detail-filled homes rather than symbolically with a book, a pen, the light on the forehead which signified intellect, and a pensive look as if in thought, were men – and they nearly always were men – of letters. Typical of this group is the portrait of the writer Sir Walter Scott in his study. When William Allan painted it in 1831, he made a record of the objects in the room, including the vase which was a gift from Byron. The nineteenth century had a love affair with the biographies of the great and good. No detail was overlooked, provided it

placed the subject in a good light, and a work like this is its visual equivalent. The extraordinary patchwork of competing patterns revealed in the living room of Robert S. Tait's portrait of Thomas Carlyle and his wife Jane in their Cheyne Row house fascinated those who were curious to see the great essayist and historian at home, and it was much praised for its realism. In 1870, Charles Mercier painted the writer Charles Reade in the Knightsbridge house he had bought with the proceeds of his successful novel *The Cloister*

and the Hearth. It is a particularly intimate picture of the writer at work at a spindly table, with four books piled on a chair and what is thought to be a picture of his mistress, the actress Mrs Laura Seymour, by his head. It is certainly her dog, Puff, on the floor. Henry Treffry Dunn recalled the setting of the watercolour he made in 1882 of the painter and poet Dante Gabriel Rossetti and the author and poet T. Watts-Dunton in the house they shared in Chelsea's Cheyne Walk: 'One of the prettiest and most curiously

Henry Treffry Dunn
Dante Gabriel Rossetti and Theodore Watts-Dunton, 1882

Paintings, mirrors, *objets d'art*, are all faithfully reproduced in this double portrait of the Pre-Raphaelite painter and poet Rossetti and the author Watts-Dunton in their home in Chelsea, one of London's artists' quarters.

Robert S. Tait

A Chelsea Interior, 1858

The nineteenth century was
fascinated by the lives of the great,
the good and the clever. This intimate
glimpse of the great thinker and writer
Thomas Carlyle at home with his wife
in Cheyne Row offers a visual equivalent
to a written description of his domestic
lifestyle. It was based on Tait's own
photographs and painstaking sketches,
a method of working that Jane Carlyle
found irksome.

Edouard Manet
Emile Zola, 1867

The interest of French artists of this period in the representation of modern life in art helped push the domestic interior into portraiture. Manet paints Zola in everyday clothes with his favourite objects on his desk and a sketch of Manet's notorious painting *Olympia* on the wall.

furnished old-fashioned parlours that I had ever seen. Mirrors and looking-glasses of all shapes, sizes and design lined the walls. Whichever way I looked I saw myself gazing at myself. What space there was left was filled up with pictures, chiefly old and of an interesting character.'[9] Towards the end of the century, this trend widened internationally to include portraits of the grandees of art, the academic painters in their studios that resembled luxuriously bohemian living rooms with their oriental rugs, carved sitters chairs, *objets d'art* and paintings on the walls.

The domestic interior was helped into portraiture by the growing interest from the 1840s in contemporary life as a subject for art. Although portraiture by its nature was tied to the present, artists needed encouragement to stress this fact. Eighteenth-century experiments in timelessness à la Reynolds by dressing subjects in vaguely classical garments, or à la Gainsborough by borrowing the costumes of an earlier century, might have seemed excessive, but its opposite, an emphasis on contemporary costume and surroundings, remained a worry to many artists of the nineteenth century.

Nowhere was the link of art and modern life discussed so brilliantly as in France. It was in his lament for the lack of invention in the 1845 Paris Salon that Baudelaire introduced his famous idea that the heroic qualities beloved by art were not solely the property of the past: 'and yet the heroism of modern life surrounds and presses upon us…we do not lack for subjects or colours with which to make epics. The painter, the true painter for whom we are searching, will be the one who can seize the epic quality of contemporary life and make us see and understand, with brush or with pencil, how great and poetic we are in our cravats and patent-leather boots.'[10]

Baudelaire's plea for cravats and patent-leather boots – the opposite of Reynolds's advice that modern dress should be avoided in portraiture – touched a chord with forward thinkers and was repeated and rephrased throughout the century. Monet's mentor, Eugène Boudin, the creator of small paintings of crowded beaches, told a friend in a letter of 1868 how he had been congratulated for 'having dared to put into paint the things and people of our time, and for

having found a way of getting the gentleman in an overcoat and his lady in a raincoat accepted…it is now making its way, and a number of young painters, chief among whom I would put Monet, find that is a subject that until now has been too much neglected. The peasants have their painters of predilection…but between ourselves these middle-class men and women, walking on the pier toward the setting sun, have they no right to be fixed on canvas, to be brought to light?'[11] The art critic Edmond Duranty, a committed supporter of the non ideal in art and a co-founder in 1856 of the short-lived journal *Le Réalisme* in support of Gustave Courbet's paintings of unidealized country people and nudes, referred to the 'realism of the frock coat, city realism' in a review of 1879.[12]

From dress it was a short step to surroundings. In 1876, Duranty wrote a pamphlet, *La Nouvelle Peinture,* timed to accompany the second Impressionist exhibition, in which he spoke about the importance of the new naturalism and the correctness of placing a sitter in his (it was understood that 'his' included 'her') workplace or environment: 'Because we cling closely to nature, we shall no longer separate the figure from the background of an apartment or of the street. In real life, the figure never appears against neutral, empty or vague backgrounds. Instead, around and behind him are furniture, fireplaces, wall hangings, or a partition that express his fortune, his class, his profession.'[13]

Manet's 1867 portrait of the author and critic Emile Zola at his desk surrounded by evidence of his artistic allegiances – the Japanese print, the reproduction of Manet's scandalous *Olympia* (1863) – is an example of what Duranty had in mind. Twenty years after this painting was made, the young English artist William Rothenstein went to visit the great author whose realist works had shocked the middle Britain of the day, and was amazed to find him living in luxury: 'His study was filled with expensive looking antiques, rich carpets and hangings, bronzes and caskets – no armour I think, but it was the kind of room in which one expected to find suits of armour. On the wall hung his portrait by Manet, in Manet's early dark manner.'[14] Perhaps at the time of Manet's painting, Zola had not become so grand a collector; or perhaps Manet and Zola decided which objects to assemble to help the portrait's message. Whatever the case, it is a useful reminder that even when a painting looks convincing, it does not necessarily mean that it offers actual reality. Although it can, of course, still offer truth.

Edgar Degas used the interior in a new and imaginative way in order to express psychological or emotional truths about his subject. The distortions of the interior of *Hélène Rouart in her Father's Study* (*c.*1886), reveal his brilliant manipulations of the composition to make his points. Everything in the room – line, colour, composition, pose – works towards creating a particular picture of this young woman. The way he has trapped her within his composition by changing the scale and position of her father's possessions, which are known from a photograph, is especially remarkable. The Chinese silk banner makes a horizontal line on top of her head and the Egyptian figures, which normally stood in a small case on his desk, have been enlarged so that their case makes a line to her left. The frames of the two paintings make a line on her right. And the chair she clings to is so enlarged it appears to imprison her. The whole effect is of a woman trapped. It is an object lesson in the difference between telling a story through precise visual detail or by means of creative distortion.

The French painter James Tissot was clearly fascinated by the look of his day and his class, although unlike his contemporaries the Impressionists, who were already formulating their fast and sketchy style in the 1860s, he persisted in a meticulous realism that had Jean-Auguste-Dominique Ingres as its hero. In 1864, he exhibited his portrait of Mlle L.L. to great acclaim. Although our eyes are drawn to the modishly dressed young woman, it does not take long to realize the role played by her setting. The traditional female contents of the room – mirror, books, table and chair – are undercut by her pose. She appears to be sitting on the table, a most unusual perch for a female portrait of the period and one that offers up a similar image of tomboyish noncomformity as her scarlet Zouave jacket, a fashion that refers to French military exploits in Africa.

Some of Tissot's happiest and most professionally successful years were spent in London, where he lived with his mistress Kathleen Newton until her death in 1882. His portrait of Frederick Gustavus Burnaby (1870), which though small makes a huge impact on all who see it, is built on a creative use of the interior. Burnaby was not only six foot four and strong as a lion, he was also a successful captain in the Royal Horse Guards and a traveller, as the breastplate and helmet, and the map on the wall, make clear. Given these facts, this is a disconcerting image. The ridiculously languid captain reclines across the painting, the red stripe on his trousers exaggerating the length of his legs. The pose is relaxed and he smokes a cigarette. Although it has been suggested that because Burnaby is in mess uniform and because it was not polite in that period to smoke in front of ladies, he must be in a male environment, we can but wonder if such a place would be so soft and pretty and furnished with sofas in floral chintz and white. The interior detail is the key to the success of this portrait, the long male legs in their dark male fabric gaining impact from the contrast with the pale soft sofa. Tissot's juxtaposition of female fabrics and male soldier makes the sitter seem doubly seductive with his almost female glamour and his masculine power and confidence. It is a *tour de force* by an artist who has used the domestic setting to disturb our expectations.

Although thousands of portraits of heads against dark backgrounds were still being made, this was not the only option for the more adventurous painters. The nineteenth century's interest in realistic detail, as obvious in fiction as in art, encouraged painters to include information about their sitters in the form of their surroundings, and by the end of the 1870s they could choose from a range of ways to achieve this aim. They could embrace the meticulous clarity of the Pre-Raphaelites or the sketchier version of reality of the Impressionists or a hybrid of both, as Tissot did with images that though painstakingly finished conveyed a spirit as daringly modern as the latest French fashions.

Somewhere between the scorn Millais met with in his realist portrait of his patron James Wyatt in 1849 and the gradual awareness of new Impressionist ideas in the 1880s, many British artists absorbed the ideas of the Pre-Rapahaelite Brotherhood and took meticulous realism to their hearts, producing some portraits of sitters in

Edgar Degas
Hélène Rouart in her Father's Study, c.1886

Degas uses the interior to add a
psychological element to his portrait of
his friend's daughter. His manipulation
of the furnishings, such as enlarging
her father's chair and ensuring the
bottom of the hanging cuts horizontally
across her head create an image of a
woman trapped.

James Tissot
Portrait of Mlle L.L., 1864

Tissot cleverly exploits the interior to help express his sitter's unconventionality. He daringly poses the young woman on the table and emphasizes this unusual positioning by setting her among traditional symbols of femininity.

Opposite: **James Tissot**
Frederick Gustavus Burnaby, 1870

Tissot's daring juxtaposition of the elegant captain and his military trappings with soft upholstery and floral fabrics creates a seductive image of almost female glamour and male power and confidence.

surroundings so painstakingly detailed that historians of interior decoration can use them for research. Just such a work is *Dulce Domum* – sweet home – painted in 1885 by Atkinson Grimshaw, an artist most famous for his moonlit scenes. The model is thought to be Grimshaw's twenty-year-old daughter Enid, the pianist perhaps her sister, and the room – for it is of equal importance in the painting – the dining room at the family home, Knostrop Hall in Yorkshire. The artist's pride in his possessions is evident in the detail with which he paints them. With its stress on the 'artistic', evidenced by Japanese fans, Chinese pots, panelling and peacock feathers, it is a textbook illustration of the interior decoration of the Aesthetic Movement.

The American portraitist John Singer Sargent, one of those artists who, like Whistler, had a high profile on three continents due to his American birth, avant-garde French connections and British patrons, experimented with a reworking of the conversation piece. His huge reputation as a portrait painter of the rich and well born was based on bravura brush strokes, dashing or glamorous versions of his sitters depending on their sex, and a conventional downplaying of the surroundings. But in 1881 he explored the idea of giving the sitters' home an important role in his portrait of the daughters of Edward Darley Boit. This work, an enlarged descendent of its eighteenth-century ancestor, shares with it the proportion of background (large) to subject (small). The girls play an almost subservient role to the atmospheric deep dark space, but the word is almost. In reality, Sargent's juxtaposition of the young sitters with the huge oriental jars and antique rug exploits the youth and fragility expressed in their pale pinafores.

Sargent returned to his interest in the conversation piece – truer to the original this time in that it was smaller – in 1899, with a portrait of Mr and Mrs Daniel Curtis, grandees of Anglo-Venetian society, with their son and daughter-in-law in their home, the Palazzo Barbaro. The resulting image of a family absorbed in its everyday activities in its everyday – albeit grand – space is a true portrait interior because the four figures have to compete with the cavernous darkness of the *salone*. However, what was easy to accept in the historical clothing of a century

earlier, proved harder for the contemporary audience. The comments were guarded and even the sitters objected. Although painted as a gift for Mrs Curtis, she declined it, partly because she thought it made her look old and partly because she thought it depicted her son in a disrespectful pose. After Mrs Curtis turned the painting down, Sargent gave it to the Royal Academy in London where in 1910 the wife of Walter Gay, the painter of interiors, saw it. 'Sargent has given the impression of a dark background, in fact has hardly done the room justice.'[15] But then Walter Gay never had to bother with the balancing act required of portrait painters who wanted to include both sitter and interior in their paintings.

Despite Mrs Gay's doubts, this Sargent-style conversation piece had a resonance for later British artists, and its usefulness as a way of adding interest to the subject survived the modernism of the twentieth century. Sargent's

William Nicholson
Sidney and Beatrice Webb, 1928–9

Commissioned by the London School
of Economics, which the Webbs
had founded in 1895, Nicholson's
painting shows the well-known
Fabian socialist couple at home
in a state of intellectual disarray.

Opposite: **John Lavery**
A Quiet Day in the Studio, 1883

Lavery's early interest in the interior is
evident in this painting of his model
relaxing before the fire and would recur
at intervals throughout his career as a
portrait painter.

Venice portrait influenced several British painters. When
William Nicholson, a reliable producer of grand portraits of
the good and great, was faced in 1928 with a commission to
paint the formidable Fabian socialists Sidney and Beatrice
Webb for the London School of Economics, he decided to
humanize them by offering an intimate look at the political
couple at home. Although they are placed either side of the
domestic hearth, have a dog and are deep in conversation,
Nicholson shows us that their minds are above domesticity
as they discuss and gesticulate, she leaning forward, he
slightly stooped, and the floor littered with folders and
scrolls of paper revealing the couple's obliviousness to
middle-class standards of tidiness. Maybe Beatrice Webb
holds her hand to the fire in a reference to the coldness of
English sitting rooms (but not too close as proof that her
mind is on higher thoughts), or maybe she is disagreeing
with a point in the document Sidney holds (they were
working on the last volume of their history of English

Poor Law). In any case, either reading is evocative of a high-
minded devotion to political beliefs.

In her diary, Beatrice Webb revealed her doubts about
the kind of portrait interior the artist was producing.
'Nicholson, the agreeable portrait painter, has been here
three weekends doing studies of us to be translated on to
the large canvas, a pleasant waste of Sidney's time and my
strength and other people's money. I doubt the result. It may
be a clever picture ("especially of the brickwork," GBS
suggests), but it will be an insignificant portrait, the figures
being too small relatively to the background and too
insignificant for the Founders' Room.'[16] With her remark
about the size of the figures and the playwright George
Bernard Shaw's disparagement of the detail of the fireplace,
she hit precisely on the doubt felt by conservative portrait
painters and public alike about any divergance from the
'head important, background less so' rule.

The fashionable Irish portrait-painter John Lavery
offers a case history of those painters, like Nicholson,
who around 1900 showed an interest in the interior and
who went on to insert it into their portraits periodically
throughout their professional lives. When he was starting
out on his career, Lavery made some paintings of what was
rapidly becoming a new subject, the model relaxing in the
studio. Although the studio interior is a subject on its own,
there are a number of examples in the nineteenth century,
beginning with the Biedermeier and Romantic artists,
where it takes on overtones of domesticity. Lavery's studio
paintings fall into this category. Far from being the excuse
for nudes one might expect, they are low-key images in
which the studio has a homely domestic air. *A Quiet Day in the
Studio* (1883) shows a model reading before a fire and *A Visit
to the Studio* (1885) shows a woman standing in an interior
with piano and low stool. In 1910, on a visit to Tangier,
Lavery painted the British Envoy, Sir Reginald Lister, in a
drawing room made big to give an elegant glamour to the
sitter. In 1913, he painted a portrait of King George V,
Queen Mary, Princess Mary, the Prince of Wales and the
living room – for there is an impressive amount of it – in
Buckingham Palace. During the First World War he painted
The Studio Window (1917), showing his wife watching German

A large proportion of Lavery's royal portrait is given over to the room, its opulent furnishings and vast size adding to the majesty of his sitters.

John Lavery
The Studio Window, 7 July 1917, 1917

An incident in the First World War inspired this painting of the artist's wife looking out through the studio window at British planes pursuing the Germans.

Opposite: **John Lavery**
The Van Dyck Room, Wilton, 1921

In the 1920s, Lavery painted a series of Impressionistic portraits of people at home, which took his interest in interiors as far as it could within the confines of portraiture.

planes being chased by the British. An incident based on fact, he initially showed his frightened wife kneeling on the window seat in front of a statuette of the Madonna, but he painted this out before presenting the painting to the Ulster Museum in 1929. In 1927, he painted the playwright George Bernard Shaw in his London home, a twentieth-century example of the men of letters genre.

It was in this decade that Lavery painted his most unusual portraits, a number of bravura impressions of the homes of the grand that successfully combined his sensitivity to the interior with his career as a fashionable portrait painter. In art-historical terms, Lavery's portrait interiors of the 1920s are descendents of the eighteenth-century conversation piece, but modernized by an impressionistic treatment that means his sitters are always threatening to disappear into the brushmarks of the interior. *The Van Dyck Room, Wilton* (1921) is all gold and paintings, sofas and light, to which the family is subordinated. Only certain kinds of patron – probably those with several

conventional portraits of themselves – would agree to be represented as little more than a glint and dab among the painting's many glints and dabs.

One of the interesting things about this group of portraits is the way it shows the continuing conflict between portraiture and background. In 1925, they were shown in an exhibition entitled *Portrait Interiors* – the earliest use of this phrase that I have come across – at the Leicester Galleries in

London. Since only two of the twenty-three sitters' names are included in the titles, it suggests that the sitters were uncomfortable with being publicly identified with the private spaces of their homes and that Lavery himself was clear which aspect of the portrait interior came first. The critic Desmond MacCarthy admired them as 'records of our times' and said that 'He shows himself in this little exhibition…as a painter of fine interiors.'[17] And when a show of Lavery's work was hung in New York the following year, the American artist Joseph Pennell wrote tartly that 'the idea of doing the millionaires surrounded by their millions was not bad.'[18] But the concept of the impressionistic portrait interior remained problematic. Could Herbert Furst have been referring to Lavery's portrait interiors when he wrote in his 1927 book, *Portrait Painting*, that Diego Velasquez's *Las Meninas* was a true portrait composition unlike the many 'interiors of today, in which the owner and his family [are] represented as mere incidents in a general aspect of walls, furniture and bric-a-brac'?[19] Clearly, the conviction that portraiture should remain an uncontaminated genre was still alive in 1927.

7 the moral interior

The development of bourgeois domesticity was an inspiration to genre painters as a fruitful source of subject matter. Genre painting had always carried moral values, but in the nineteenth century the importance of the home and all the issues surrounding it to do with family life resulted in paintings of the interior that present us with snapshots of conventional belief.

Starting with the fifteenth-century Netherlandish paintings of Mary holding Jesus, the painted domestic interior had early staked its claim to be a female habitat. Even when Mary is shown out-of-doors, it is a domestic exterior she sits in, the enclosed garden that signals her untested sexuality. The comparable biblical stories involving men, such as the Last Supper and the Presentation in the Temple, are set in public not domestic spaces.

Joseph, the one man who might be expected to inhabit an interior, tended to be left out of images of the Holy Family until the Counter-Reformation returned him to Mary's side; an edict of the Council of Trent in 1563 involved artists in bringing the holy stories back to ordinary people's understanding. A rare instance of Christ in a house, the story of Martha and Mary, is actually a woman's story whose moral is to content her with her domestic lot. The hardworking Martha longs to dispute with the men as her sister Mary does, sitting at the feet of Christ. Jesus counsels her that she serves God through her housewifery. Velasquez did a painting of a sullen Martha being admonished by Mary while through a door, in a mirror or a painting on the wall – it is not clear – Christ raises his hand in benediction to the women at his feet. The moral is obvious but the glory of the work is the still life on the kitchen table, an assembly of classically Spanish ingredients – eggs, fish, garlic, pepper – and the red knuckled hands of Martha as she pounds the pestle in the copper pot. The stress on domesticity signals this is a work specifically aimed at women.

The identification of home as a woman's place was expanded in pictorial terms by the seventeenth-century Dutch. Firstly, as the site of the family, with images showing women in interiors relaxing, working, with children or with servants tidying. Pieter de Hooch's *A Mother and Child with its Head in her Lap* (see p.11) is typical. Done about four years after his marriage in 1654, during his great years as a painter of Delft interiors, it shows a little girl with her head buried in the lap of her mother who is delousing the child's hair. Secondly, as the site of all the female rituals from courtship to motherhood. And thirdly, as a place of recreation between the sexes. The home was the legitimate way for respectable women to interact with men (although for men, of course, it was only one of the ways). The Dutch paintings of men holding their wine glasses up to the light and women playing music in comfortable surroundings established the domestic interior as one of the few places in art where men and women of the polite classes could be shown together in ways unmediated by historical or religious themes. True to their time, many of the Dutch paintings, particularly those in which a man and woman are shown singing or playing a musical instrument, carry a finger-pointing moral but it was a general kind of moral, related to the world of proverbs (the lazy/good housewife) or stock themes of a mildly risqué nature (an invitation to sexual misbehaviour). This chapter

examines how this tradition developed and changed in the nineteenth century to enable the interior to be used to consider issues of contemporary domesticity instead of making a general moral point.

In the early 1800s, women's role in the home was on the brink of change. The new industries and ways of organizing the economy that resulted from the Industrial Revolution meant that the integration of home and workplace was replaced by a division between home and factory or office, leaving the wife at home with the servants and children. (Of course, for the servants, the home was a workplace.) With the expansion of the middle classes, a new set of social expectations came into being. Women became the keepers

of the home, while the men went out to work. The interior's identity as a female space was underpinned by an impregnable social, ethical and religious code that assigned a set of roles, rights and behaviour to women. Men had their interiors, too – the club, the garret, the bar, the workplace – but the home was a private world where women had their base. At its best, the home gave women their own sphere of influence; at its worst, it ensured they were its prisoners, subject to social expectations and the men of the family.

Thomas Gisborne, an evangelical clergyman, explains woman's power in a Christian conduct book, *An Enquiry into the Duties of the Female Sex*, first published in 1797 but still going

Diego Velasquez
Kitchen Scene with Christ in the House of Martha and Mary, c.1618

While most biblical stories involving men take place in public spaces, those concerning women are set in the home. Although she longs to sit at Christ's feet disputing with the men, Martha is encouraged to be content with her domestic lot.

strong in 1847 with the publication of the fourteenth edition. 'Home is the centre round which the influence of every married woman is accumulated. It is there that she will naturally be known and respected the most;….Home, therefore, is the place where the pattern which she exhibits in personal manners, in domestic arrangements, and in every branch of her private conduct will be more carefully observed….Home too is the place where she will possess peculiar means of doing good, among the humbler classes of society.' Like many others, Gisborne believed that the habits of metropolitan life were a bar to the cultivation of connubial happiness: 'The husband and the wife are systematically kept asunder. Separate establishments, separate sets of acquaintances, separate amusements, all conspire to render them first strangers, and afterwards indifferent to each other.' His solution was to suggest that the wife's duty was to render home, 'by the winning charms of her behaviour, attractive and delightful for her husband….Let the cheerful tranquillity of domestic pleasure stand forward to supply the place of trifling and disturbing festivity abroad.'[1]

For most people, attitudes such as these, stemming from the teachings of the Church, were a western phenomenon accepted as uncritically as the Bible. In mid-century France, Louise d'Alq wrote: 'Man does not need to come back home to find a second self; that he could find at his club or at a café.'[2] In England in 1870, J.W. Kirton wrote with religious intent and with the lower classes in mind in *Happy Homes and How to Make Them* that he wanted to 'help to make the homes of England the brightest spots in the world, and so become the foretaste of the world above'. For Kirton, it was the public house that was the enemy of the home: 'it is the publican's special business to draw people away from their homes, and induce them to spend their time and money in his house.'[3]

The middle-class home had become a sacred space and woman its priestess. The woman in her domestic setting was credited with almost superhuman powers to spread morality, sweetness and light. The message of the cult of the home was spread via the rapidly developing press and publishing industries and absorbed by an increasingly literate population. The home was felt to be better and purer than the male world of work, a special space presided over by women, a delicate class of beings possessed of kindness, sensitivity and piety. As the site for feminine virtues and a place of tranquillity, family and friends, it was presented as a sanctuary to which the man could return with pleasure and relief. 'While it is a man's place to be out, it is a woman's place to be at HOME.'[4] Phrases like this reverberated through the nineteenth century. The theories that were developed at this time have a rococo expansiveness, all curlicues and encrustations of justifications, explanations and examples of why a woman's place was in the home, which itself was weighted with ideas of safety, warmth and relaxation.

The domestic interior reached one of its artistic pinnacles in mid-nineteenth-century England. The development of the idea of the home as a frame for the wife and mother made it an inevitable setting for a group of paintings that were the artistic equivalent of the long Victorian novels which dealt with contemporary issues. With Hogarth as their spiritual father, painters such as Robert Braithwaite Martineau and Augustus Egg told their tales to fascinated audiences. Loved and cursed in equal measure, these paintings still draw audiences today. Admirers are fascinated by their detail and the tales they tell, reading them like silent movies; opponents despise them for their narrative values, which they feel have nothing to do with art. From the perspective of the subject of this book, they show the home making its way into art as a modern moral subject.

These paintings reveal a frequently camouflaged truth about the mid-nineteenth-century woman and the home. While ostensibly the ruler of her domestic kingdom, memorably described by the poet Coventry Patmore as the angel of the house and by hundreds of others as its guiding light, heart and moral centre, the reality was that in law the woman was far less powerful. Until the Married Women's Property Acts of 1870 and 1882 allowed a woman some control over her own property and responsibility for her own debts, she had few rights. This meant that while the woman may have ruled the home in the sense of organizing its functions, food and comfort, it was the man who had the power that went with legal ownership.

In 1864, Robert Kerr's *The Gentleman's House, or, How to Plan English Residences from the Parsonage to the Palace* appeared, the first of many editions which continued throughout the century. Its title makes the ideology transparent. The concept of a lady's house was just not possible in a period when a man was expected to support his wife. Even if through marriage the money came from her, it could not be publicly expressed in those terms.

A fascinating aspect of Kerr's book for modern readers is the way he reveals that only parts of the house were the woman's province. He does not come out and openly discuss the gendered spaces of the house – not that he would ever have expressed it in those terms. Instead, his assumptions slip into the text: 'If the family be distinguished for hospitality of one sort, the development of the Dining-room and its accessories, and also of the Kitchen department, must be a prominent feature of the plan; if, on the other hand, hospitality be equally great, but in another form, it is the Drawing-room and the ladies' department which must be made to excel.'⁵ According to Kerr, the drawing room was 'the Lady's apartment essentially, being the modern form of the Lady's Withdrawing Room or perfected chamber of medieval plan. It should be south facing, so the ladies can enjoy the open air and its decoration should in contrast to the dining room "be entirely ladylike".'⁶ He lists the desirable drawing-room qualities as cheerfulness, refinement of elegance and lightness. 'Ladies receive calls there in the afternoon; the family and guests assemble there before dinner; ladies withdraw there after dinner.'⁷ The novelty of Kerr's book was it could be scaled up or down according to the reader's circumstances. The bedroom, for example, was shared although a dressing table for the lady was a necessity. As soon as space permitted, however, the man was to move his belongings out to his own dressing room, leaving the bedroom to the lady. If space allowed, the woman was also allocated the boudoir as her sitting room and business room, as well as the morning room, which as it sounds, could be occupied by the ladies in the morning. Men had the dining room, due to the 'pitiable resources to which some gentlemen are driven, even in their own houses, in order to be able to enjoy the pestiferous luxury of a cigar.'⁸

Of course, in a bigger establishment, a gentleman would be allowed a room in which to smoke all day if he so wished.

Despite all the words written in the nineteenth century in praise of the woman as the heart of the home, the truth was that her entitlement was less secure than the man's. For a man, the home was an investment in property and a refuge from the world outside, a place where ownership entitled him to find peace, pleasure and comfort. Her position was more precarious and depended on the financial support, impeccable behaviour and belief in the contemporary scheme of things on the part of the man. Domestic life with all its contradictions was at the core of bourgeois Victorian life.

It is in genre painting, with its devotion to the depiction of everyday life, that we find some interesting explorations of these contradictions. The eighteenth-century argument for genre paintings as modern histories took root and, combined with the growth of a middle-class picture-buying public, became acceptable. Paintings of the everyday life of the new middle classes at work or at play, indoors or outdoors, became so popular that by mid-century history painting no longer held its exalted position. This was as true in Russia as it was in France, to take as an example two countries at very different stages of artistic development. Finding a 'good' subject for this type of modern genre haunted mid-century artists. In his autobiography, the English artist William Powell Frith, whose famous *Derby Day* depicted a slice of 1850s life in all its multi-layered complexity, recalled offering large rewards for suggestions, an unsuccessful gesture, it turned out.

If genre was the vehicle for painted explorations of Victorian daily life, then realism was the fuel. The elaborate ideology displayed in the paintings needed meticulous realism to bring it to life. Artists' memoirs of the period recall the lengths to which they went to ensure that their images looked 'real' and that their story was 'true'. The artist's imagination lay behind the scene on the canvas but to tell the story to the public, the setting and the props had to be as realistic and recognizable as the viewers' living rooms. Tramps were rounded up to be used as models, only to find themselves doused in flea powder and stood on brown paper

William Holman Hunt
The Awakening Conscience, 1853

Every item in Hunt's painting underlines the moral message of the kept woman's dawning horror at her situation.

Opposite: **Robert Braithwaite Martineau**
The Last Day in the Old Home, 1862

Betrayed by the feckless behaviour of the head of the house, the women are forced to leave the comfort and protection of their home.

before they were allowed into the studio. Shops were searched for the perfect chair for a particular setting. It was believed that the more realistic the painting, the more convincing the art work. It is a belief sneered at as naïve today by the same people who never question the lengths gone to by the designers of TV dramatizations of nineteenth-century novels.

It was the English who took the modern moral subject most seriously. We are right to view these mid-century storytelling interiors with respect. When William Holman Hunt set *The Awakening Conscience* of 1853 in the newly furnished parlour, complete with cheap rosewood piano, of a kept woman, he aroused such shocked cries from his Victorian audience that the art critic and Pre-Raphaelite supporter John Ruskin felt compelled to quell them with a letter to *The Times*. 'There is not a single object in that room, – common, modern, vulgar…but it become tragical if rightly read,' he wrote in his mission to convince the readers of the artist's serious intent. 'The furniture so carefully painted, even to the last vein of the rosewood – is there nothing to be learnt from that terrible lustre of it, from its fatal newness; nothing there that has the old thoughts of home upon it, or that is even to become a part of home? Those embossed books, vain and useless, – they are also new, – marked with no happy wearing of beloved leaves,…the picture above the fireplace, with its single drooping figure – the woman taken in adultery.'[9] Holman Hunt's crime was to present moral depravity on the gallery's walls. His intention of showing the woman's dawning awareness of her wickedness was undercut by a setting whose realism, at least to a portion of his male spectators, was shockingly out of place at the Royal Academy, a temple of high art which was visited by their mothers, wives and daughters.

The domestic interior lies at the heart of Martineau's *Last Day in the Old Home* (1862), which is presented in full Hogarthian detail to make sure we understand the tale. The painting is about the destruction of the female habitat at the hands of those entrusted with its upkeep. The female occupants weep or look distressed because their place of safety has been gambled away by the husband of the seated woman, whose young son ominously lifts his glass in

Augustus Egg
Past and Present No.1, 1858

The wife's adultery has destroyed the home it is the woman's duty to uphold. The repercussions of her act are symbolized by the precarious house of cards her children are building on a chair.

emulation of his father. Martineau supplies us with a great deal of domestic detail. The comfortable room is stuffed with books (women were identified with novel reading in the period) as well as evidence of the family's history. To underline the tragedy, workmen can be glimpsed through the doorway on the right removing items to sell at auction to pay off the father's debts. The inclusion of a painting within a painting traditionally offers a visual commentary on the main event: Martineau places a painting of a shipwreck on the wall as a metaphor for the situation.

In the first scene of Augustus Egg's *Past and Present* (1858), the carefully presented comfortable home has been desecrated by the woman lying on the floor. An intercepted note held by her husband has revealed her adultery while the house of cards built by the couple's innocent children symbolically tumbles down. In the centre of the painting a mirror reflects an open door, the door through which has entered the sin that has defiled the family, the door through which the wife and mother must leave. This painting, and its two companion scenes, illustrate by means of interiors what happens when the marriage contract is violated: in a sober bedroom her by-now adolescent daughters wonder where, under the moon, their mother lies; under the same moon, a Thames bridge shelters their mother and her illegitimate baby. It could not be clearer that while men own the home, it is the woman's habitat and although men are responsible for providing the home, the woman is responsible for keeping it pure.

Not all paintings are as bleak as these. George Elgar Hicks's *Woman's Mission: Companion of Manhood*, exhibited in 1863, is a textbook example of the Victorian wifely ideal with its image of a woman supporting her husband who has received news of a bereavement in the morning post. This is a painting where the details surrounding the figures help lodge the couple's situation vividly in the mind. The white tablecloth, the round table pleasantly set for breakfast, the fur hearthrug, the flowers and fabrics that surround the couple are put there to suggest the special female ability to make home a haven of soft textures, warmth and comfort.

The new Victorian technology of iron and glass which encouraged the hothouses where the great families raised their rare and out-of-season foods and flowers led to the more

George Elgar Hicks
*Woman's Mission: Companion
of Manhood*, 1863

Hunt's depiction of the domestic
interior as comfortable and enclosed
presents it as a haven against the
stresses of the outside world. The
woman with her sympathy and
support is its living breathing spirit,
finding her happiness in helping her
husband through his grief, indicated
by the black-edged letter.

James Tissot
*The Conservatory (The Rivals), c.*1875–8

The conservatory is an ambiguous space in Victorian art and fiction. Neither indoors nor outdoors, its balmy air encourages moral flexibility, as can be seen in the mutually engrossed couple near the background palms. The foreground scene, by contrast, is more innocent.

Opposite: **Pavel Fedotov**
The Major's Proposal, 1848

Inspired by Hogarth, Fedotov grounds his painting, a huge success in its day, in a Russian bourgeois interior. The beautiful young woman is unwilling to meet the swaggering older man who will solve the family's financial problems.

domesticated conservatories of the middle classes. The conservatory was a slightly risqué place for meetings between young men and women. The balmy air held a taint of moral flexibility and paintings set there often display hothouse emotions as well as flowers. Tissot's *The Conservatory (The Rivals)* foregrounds twin sisters dressed alike in innocent blue who drink tea with a man and an older woman while in the background amid the palms a mature man and woman relate to each other more intimately and intensely.

It was not only the English who wished to explore the ideology of the home in the nineteenth century. There is evidence of interest in female-centred subject matter in

other countries, although rarely treated with such seriousness as in England. In Russia, Pavel Fedotov, a wealthy amateur painter and admirer of Hogarth, created a stir at the 1848–9 Academy exhibition with his realistic and satirical works, *The Major's Proposal* and *The Fussy Bride,* both dealing with the centrality of marriage in a woman's life. In *The Fussy Bride,* a humpbacked suitor kneels before an ageing woman and in *The Major's Proposal* the beautiful daughter of an impoverished merchant home is loathe to meet the louche older suitor who will repair the family's fortunes. Although subject paintings, all the details of the rooms were based on life. Fedotov was a realist: 'very little of my work –

about a tenth – takes place in the studio,' which I take to mean that he saw himself as a student of life.[10]

In Italy, the Macchiaioli group of artists, active between 1850 and 1870, were committed to the portrayal of contemporary issues, an interest that sometimes, though not always, included the depiction of daily life. Their driving force was doubly revolutionary, artistically against the tradition-bound teaching of the Florence Academy of Art and politically for the cause of unification of the Italian states. Their very name, like that of the Pre-Raphaelites, refers back to early Renaissance practices, for *macchia* is the word for the patches of colour that Renaissance artists set down before the finishing details of their frescoes.

Macchiaioli paintings of women in interiors have a particular freshness that sits midway between the no-comment tendency of the Impressionism they foreshadowed and the moralizing of mid-century genre which did not attract them. It is as if these artists are seeing women in their

Adriano Cecioni
*Interior with a Figure, c.*1867

An intriguing image in terms of meaning – perhaps she is a servant betrayed by the master – which shows that by mid-century detailed depictions of contemporary interiors were a feature of paintings across Europe.

domestic settings for the first time and with a fresh eye. *At the Piano* is an example of Piero Dini's interest in the early 1870s in capturing the charm of domestic scenes. Adriano Cecioni's *Interior with Figure* (*c.*1867) is mysterious – is she sad, is she praying, is she hiding? But the room is clarity itself with its blue wallpaper, pinkish tiled floor and hand-trimmed bedspread. Cecioni is better known as a sculptor and the chronicler of the Macchiaioli but a memorial essay speaks of one of his group of paintings set in domestic interiors in which, in the interests of domestic realism, the main player, placed directly in the viewer's line of sight, was 'a beautiful chamber pot', which 'made the purists shout so much that no one wanted to discuss the pictorial qualities of the canvas'.[11] A more subtle use of the bourgeois interior occurs in Odoardo Borrani's painting *Red Shirt Seamstresses* of 1863. The solemn seamstresses in almost prayerful attitudes who sit silently working in the tranquillity of a bourgeois room are in fact making red shirts for Garibaldi's soldiers. The enclosure of the contemporary interior protected from the outside world by elaborate window draperies underlines the nun-like qualities of the women, whose poses refer back to Renaissance prototypes. The artist clearly finds the idea of domestic revolutionaries inspirational.

What had seemed so monolithic and persuasive in the first half of the century began to crumble as the second half neared its end. In the last decades of the century an explosion of plays and fiction began to question the earlier certainties. The home, the relationships within it and its relationship to the wider world became a subject of great interest to such playwrights as Ibsen, Strindberg and Chekhov, and to novelists such as the American Charlotte Perkins Gilman whose story, *The Yellow Wallpaper* (1899), is an example of a woman driven to madness by the limitations of domesticity.

The concept of the psychological interior, which foregrounds a kind of unspecified unease, has been formulated as a kind of visual equivalent to this literature. Art historians have argued that several of Vuillard's domestic interiors reveal the tensions of his family life, but in 1868–9 Degas painted a work that prefigured these, often referred to as *The Rape* but entitled more conservatively in

Odoardo Borrani
Red Shirt Seamstresses, 1863

The poses have a Renaissance
tranquillity but the room is
contemporary with its objects,
pictures and elaborately draped
windows. Although not obviously
political, the women are sewing red
shirts for Garibaldi's soldiers who
were fighting to unify Italy.

Edgar Degas
Interior, 1868–9

Depictions of the domestic interior became more complex as the century moved on. The murky light, the exaggerated recession of the bed, rug and floorboards, and the unanswered questions of the man and woman make Degas' painting brim with an atmosphere of psychological unease.

the Philadelphia Museum of Art's catalogue as *Interior*. It seems like *lèse majesté* to taint so avant-garde an artist with the genre label, but he himself referred to it as his genre painting and the work is definitely about something, even though the 'about' is unclear.[12] A controlled and clothed man stands with his back to the door; a dishevelled and distressed woman crouches against a chair; and the room, most definitely part of the story, is obviously a bedroom. The whole scene, which is the subject of academic dispute, may refer to the miserable wedding night of Thérèse to Laurent, her husband's murderer, from Emile Zola's novel *Thérèse Raquin* (1868). It conveys psychological unease through the manipulation of scale, the unexplained relationship of the couple – Egg and Martineau would have draped the room

with visual clues – and the intimate interior. It is not strictly a moral subject, because the meaning is obscure and modern artists such as Degas prided themselves on not being tellers of tales: that was the old art. But undeniably it rouses our curiosity by asking questions it does not answer. It is a teasing painting, almost as if the artist wants it both ways, to be recognized for modernity of technique yet also to engage the viewer by offering a subject that intrigues.

The mood is as important as the story in *The Rape*, a development that adds new possibilities to the presentation of the interior. In Belgium, a sub-genre of atmospheric interiors arose in the last years of the century, sometimes attached to a story but more often just an exploration of the strangeness that can be evoked by looking sideways at the most familiar aspects of our lives. A group of artists including Xavier Mellery, Georges Le Brun and Léon Spilliaert created images of ordinary rooms that in their hands can be seen as examples of *fin-de-siècle* mystery recast in terms of the interior. Mellery was fascinated by shadowy staircases while Le Brun drew a man disappearing past a door in *The Man Walking By*.

As the taste for moralized genre weakened, the artists moved with the times. Though the subject in an interior remained, the narrative was played down and the works were characterized by a sketchier treatment. William Quiller Orchardson followed these principles, with the result that detail loses out to the big impression. In *The First Cloud* (1887), a huge expanse of parquet flooring is equivalent to the rift between the newly married couple. *Mariage de Convenance* (1883) shows a young wife and her older husband in a state of some estrangement, metaphorically placed at opposite ends of a long dining table. The title of its

William Quiller Orchardson
Mariage de Convenance, 1883

This is still an interior, but artistic ideas have moved to something sketchier than mid-Victorian detail. Orchardson's interest is in the tension between the couple, symbolized by the long tabletop that separates them.

companion piece, *Mariage de Convenance – After!* (1886), shows Hogarth's influence on the Victorians. In England in the 1890s, there was a vogue for something called the problem picture, described as 'ambiguous, and often slightly risqué, paintings of modern life which invited multiple, equally plausible interpretations'.[13] John Collier was its main exponent, pandering to the English fondness for a story, but labelling it with a title that confused rather than clarified. His version of *Mariage de Convenance* (1907), for example, was set in a bedroom containing two women, one standing confidently hand on hip, the other weeping by the bed. He appreciated the role played by the interior: 'having got my characters, their attitudes and their expressions, I next consider their environment, for they cannot possibly be real unless that environment is natural to them.'[14]

This interest in the right environment for the right subject lingered on in England. Even a modernist like Sickert, who was at home in France and a friend of Degas, succumbed. Despite his determination to prevent accusations of storytelling by either not naming, or multi-naming his paintings of a clothed man and a naked woman in a murky bedroom, for example *The Camden Town Murder or What Shall We Do For the Rent* (c.1908), these are first cousins of Collier's problem pictures. Sickert's fluent and engaging writings about art explain how he liked to form his nudes with glimmers. By painting in the manner of the French Impressionists, and in particular Degas, he is expounding the new painterly values; but by painting clothed men and naked women on iron beds in spartan rooms for an audience given to looking for a story, he is arousing our curiosity about the subject. Again, the artist as tease.

By the 1880s, it was commonplace, particularly in the northern European countries, to see cottage interiors of the rural poor on gallery walls. Artists had traditionally painted the poor as picturesque or, as was the case with the seventeenth-century Dutch, as examples of feckless living, but it was not until the last third of the nineteenth century that attempts were made to show the lower classes realistically in their homes.

A handful of artists took this very seriously and tried to tell the truth about the sorry condition of the poor. Though such works had little appeal for ordinary buyers, they attracted huge critical attention at the Salon exhibitions and were often bought by institutions. One of the most famous, *The Doctor* (1891) by Luke Fildes, shows a doctor watching a little girl through the crisis of her illness. So poor is the family that her bed has been made up of two wooden chairs placed side by side. In the interests of realism, Fildes spent a week sketching fishermen's cottages at Hope Cove in Devon. 'From these sketches a full-size interior of a cottage was built in a corner of the studio in Melbury Road, with rafters and walls and a window – this last part of one of the studio windows – through which the light of dawn would come, for he had set himself an "artistic exercise" which was to record how dawn and lamplight would mingle.'[15] It showed doctors in so good a light that prints of it could be found in doctors' surgeries all over the United States until the 1950s.

Far more popular and numerous were the paintings of the hard-working rural poor. By the 1880s, there was a widely accepted theory of the physical and moral degeneration of urban workers compared with their rural counterparts. This theory took hold at the same time as the

Luke Fildes
The Doctor, 1891

In the interests of accuracy, Fildes built a cottage interior in his London studio for what became a famous late Victorian image. This painting captures two concerns of its day, the plight of the deserving poor and the heroism of those who helped them.

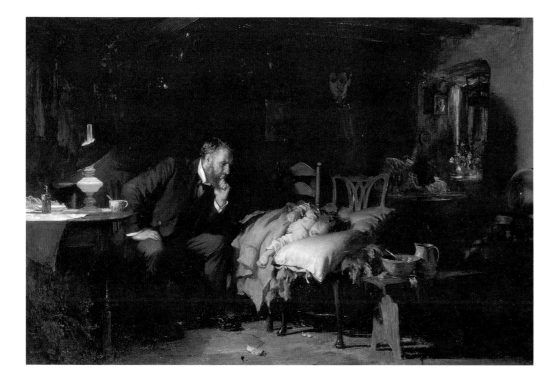

growth of artists' colonies, a legacy of the Impressionist belief in painting in the open air, where artists migrated in the summer months. Here, in the country or more often by the sea, painters worked outdoors, finding picturesque subjects for the paintings they would take back to the city to work up for exhibition in their national Salon shows.

What the painters saw – in common with the fashionable thinking of the time – was the value of the simple life. In England, such concerns manifested themselves in the arts in what could be called a wave of aesthetic nationalism, which in literature produced Thomas Hardy's chronicles of the passing ways of the countryside, in architecture the domestic revival, in music the collecting of folk tunes, and in paintings the works of the Newlyn School, an artists' colony on the coast of Cornwall.

Some very beautiful cottage interiors were painted in this period, as always with a female focus and often explored through the great events of female lives. The masterpiece of the leading Newlyn painter, Stanhope Forbes, was *The Health of the Bride* (1889), based on a local cottage interior and modelled by the village inhabitants. The previous year, visitors to the Royal Academy were impressed by Frank

Stanhope Forbes
The Health of the Bride, 1889

In this large painting of a working-class wedding in the artists' colony of Newlyn, Cornwall, Forbes continues the tradition of seeing the interior as the site of great events in women's lives. This is a modern version of the history painting, the moral values traditionally expressed through biblical and historical events replaced by the hardwork and modesty of the nineteenth-century fisherfolk.

Frank Bramley
The Hopeless Dawn, 1888

Bramley's huge painting uses the breaking dawn entering the interior, usually a sign of hope and resurrection, to speak of the woman's despairing realization that her fisherman husband will not return. The greys of this Newlyn masterpiece are enlivened only by the red of the young wife's hair.

Bramley's masterpiece *The Hopeless Dawn*, a large work of moving intimacy in which he used subtle tones to create the dawn light that reveals the meagre furnishings of the cottage. Despite the Victorian sentimentality of the old woman comforting the young wife whose husband has been claimed by the stormy sea visible outside the window, this is an image that moves the viewer through its solemn greys and chilly light. It caused the poet and critic Alice Meynell, sister of the renowned military painter Elizabeth Butler, to wrestle with the new French doctrine forbidding pictures to tell a story, which by this time was how Impressionism was perceived. Happily, she decided that though it was 'painted for the sake of the profound human interest, it might, for the great beauty of its execution and perfect sincerity with which all the truths of light and surface are presented have been painted for the sake of these alone.'[16]

These paintings represent one of the interior's moments of triumph. Although conventionally described as genre paintings, their size and the thinking of the day suggest that they were intended as modern history paintings, updated examples of Reynolds's Grand Style outlined in Discourse 4. Impressionism and its variations may have seduced the British avant-garde, but Reynolds was still looked to for authority by all those who believed, as R.A.M Stevenson argued in *The Art of Velasquez* (1895), that the Impressionists had done nothing that the Spaniard had not done first. The seventeen books on Reynolds published between 1870 and 1900 that are listed in the British Library index show the great man remaining influential a century after his death.

As the century drew to a close and genre lost its moral mission, it began to be replaced by paintings of people in interiors that offered little in the way of psychological or moral message. Some of these interiors are clad in historical dress – the clothes and minutely detailed interiors of the Regency were popular – in an attempt to make them look more decorative to the picture-buying public. They are as pointless as they are picturesque with their flounces, flowers and polished furniture. What is particularly odd about them is that despite the authentic dress and decor, they always look Victorian and the activities they portray – reading, chatting, making music – look Victorian too. This is even the

case with the classical interiors of the Royal Academician Lawrence Alma-Tadema whose meticulous research always ends up displaying the glorious inauthenticity of a biblical epic by Cecil B. De Mille. *A Silent Greeting* (1889), shows a Roman soldier tip-toeing out of a marble-floored room in order not to wake the young woman in whose lap he has left a bunch of flowers. A pretty redhead, she relaxes in sleep on a hard, severely Roman-looking sofa softened with pillows. Such paintings are a byway in the history of art which few bother to explore. It is not hard to see why: they are backdated from an era that is already backdated to us. And yet, this Roman-Victorian hybrid offers proof that the new subject of the domestic interior was now firmly established.

Probably thousands of images were painted between 1880 and 1910 of men and women in contemporary interiors, the painted equivalent of the drawing-room comedies that could be seen at the theatre. Rowland Holyoake's *The Connoisseur* of *c*.1893 is typical. It shows a man in a fashionable Aesthetic interior examining his collection of prints and drawings while ignoring his lovely wife, a living work of art in her green column of a dress. This is the kind of painting that is only noted in the histories of interior decoration, where it is prized for its detail. It carries no moral, beyond the kind that gives the spectator a wry chuckle, and it rouses no painful thoughts in the spectator. Instead, it offered a sanitized version of the domestic life of those who viewed it and as such it represents a new entry in the subject matter of art.

Lawrence Alma-Tadema
A Silent Greeting, 1889

By the end of the nineteenth century, the domestic interior was firmly established as a subject that needed no message beyond a quirky twist. Here, the interior is classical, with a Roman soldier leaving a bouquet in the lap of a very Victorian-looking sleeping woman.

Rowland Holyoake

*The Connoisseur, c.*1893

Genre paintings of domestic interiors became as common as drawing-room comedies by 1900. The joke here is that the connoisseur of images has no time for the statuesque beauty of his own wife.

8 the artist's own interior

Gustaf Cederström
An Interior with a Woman Reading by a Table, 1897

In the last two decades of the nineteenth century, Scandinavian artists produced many paintings of women in interiors. The depiction of the pleasure of light, of comfort, of domestic life and of interior decoration as personal expression has here replaced the need to tell a story. Cederström's sitter is probably his daughter Carola, aged twenty.

A new subject appears in painting in the second half of the nineteenth century: the artist's home. By 1870, their own domestic interiors and what went on in them had become of interest to an increasing number of artists, yet one more aspect of the depiction of daily life that was so strong a strand of nineteenth-century painting. For the first time, artists used their own homes, their own lives and their own families as a jumping-off point for their paintings.

There had been earlier examples at the start of the century, such as the paintings of their studios made by German artists of the Biedermeier. Studio paintings appear with increasing frequency in the nineteenth century, but they are usually scenes of students or masters surrounded by the models, casts, busts and easels that make the studio so fascinating to outsiders. The Biedermeier studio interiors with their small domestic windows, their peace and quiet, their little vases of flowers, stress the homely element above the artistic and seem to talk of personal matters. Though not for public consumption, Adolph Menzel's oil sketches of the 1840s are precursors too, as we know from his habit of being late for meals because of his desire to sketch a domestic moment.

Women of course had always used their interiors for inspiration, not just in watercolour, but in their oils as well. Before the middle of the nineteenth century, the history of the subjects most women chose to paint shows that it was nearly always those which did not require an elaborate studio setup, the necessity of drawing out-of-doors (a sure way to attract unwelcome attention), or the experience of the life classes to which they had no access before the end of the nineteenth century. The flowers, portraits and still lifes they chose to paint were all subjects that were domestic and accessible. Unfortunately, they were also low in the hierarchy of genres, which did the women no service with the critics.

However, the contemporary life which became increasingly interesting to artists after mid-century helped raise the status of these 'women's' subjects. The expansion of the pleasures and recreations of family life meant that the home could no longer be dismissed as 'just' a place for women and its new importance as subject matter meant that women artists were no longer disadvantaged by subjects previously forced on them by circumstance and training. The education of the women Impressionists of the 1870s coincided with these new ideas about daily life as subject matter, which meant they could paint the surroundings in which they lived their lives with no apparent detriment to their desire to be taken seriously. (The fact that most critics of the time saw them as painting 'women's subjects' – even in the face of the evidence that men were painting them too – is another story.)

I do not want to suggest that the Impressionist women painted only their households. Impressionism's original *raison d'être* was painting out-of-doors and the women accepted this completely. Attitudes were changing in the 1860s and 1870s, and though the conventions governing the lives of women made it harder for women than for men to set up easels outdoors and start to draw and paint, some did manage it, helped by the growing agreement about women having a right to express their talent and the opening of art academies

The domestic rituals of women were of great interest to Degas. This home visit of the chiropodist to the sheet-swatched young girl is a beautiful and unusual example of the private life of women entering art.

to meet that need. They inhabited two worlds, the domestic and the professional, as the men did, but their professional world was a little more confined than that of the men, though not necessarily one they despised or railed against. Like Renoir picturing women in the street, Degas at the milliner, Manet in the cafés and bars of Paris, the Impressionist women also painted scenes from outside the home. Mary Cassatt did a number of paintings of women going out and about, driving a horse and cart, sitting in a box at the opera, although unlike the men's images, Cassatt's tend to a closeup focus on her female subjects. And sometimes the women Impressionists' outdoors seems a little tamer than the men's: a park, the garden, or the view from a window that Berthe Morisot painted on her honeymoon on the Isle of Wight.

Nonetheless, the home, its rituals and its inhabitants held a central place for the women in the group. Cassatt and Morisot painted their households throughout their careers; and the less-known Eva Gonzalès (who died after childbirth in her early thirties) and Marie Bracquemond (who gave up art in her thirties) painted their friends and family. Mary Cassatt has left a legacy of the female social rituals of the period. With its comfortable sofa, grand fireplace, polished silver and delicately controlled gestures, *Tea* (1879–80) is good manners itself. The men painted domestic rituals too – *The Pedicure* (1873) by Degas shows a sheet-swathed young woman on a sofa receiving the chiropodist's attentions – but men could select their subjects from anywhere they wished (Degas' subject

Mary Cassatt
Tea, 1879–80

The home and its rituals had a central place in the subject matter of Impressionist painters. Cassatt's image of 'le five o'clock' dignifies the world of women with its serious treatment of the decorous young ladies.

may have been a professional model), a freedom less available to women.

Although technically as interesting as the bourgeois interiors produced by the men in the group – Berthe Morisot's watercolour-inspired technique of thin little flurries of colour is a most individual contribution to Impressionism – there is a different feel to them. They are often presented with an intriguing slant, which comes from their different social standpoint. As we saw with Morisot's mirror and window paintings, the women painters dignify these subjects with their sympathetic understanding.

Most of the reasons why male artists started to look at their own domestic interiors at this time have been discussed already: the new importance of the home as a place of comfort; the existence of a middle-class buying public that did not want heroics or suffering in the images they put on their walls; the development of modern life as a subject for art – it was only a short step from Baudelaire's advice to stroll around the city as if it were one's empire to looking upon one's home in the same way; the decline of narrative – by the 1860s, the theories that would result in French Impressionism killed off the picture which told a story for any artist who wished to be seen as up-to-date; the advent of new techniques – the old hierarchies of subject matter and of boundaries between subjects were irrelevant to the new way of painting, which downplayed traditional ideas of composition, careful tonal values and smooth finish in favour of capturing the moment. Freed from the need for a subject, the dabby brushstrokes and adventurous colour of Impressionism showed that the making of a painting was as important as its subject.

Artists stopped genuflecting to the rules and felt free to paint what they liked. To begin with, their dedication to the practice of catching the effects of outdoor light meant that exteriors outnumbered interiors. But Impressionism's enchantment with light and the pleasures of daily life ensured that works of pleasant domesticity were also painted. As Duranty argued, 'Our lives take place in rooms and in streets, and rooms and streets have their own special laws of light and visual language.'[1] Sometimes I think the word 'rooms' has got lost in that statement.

Claude Monet
The Luncheon, 1868

Many artists found their own domestic situation a fruitful source of subject matter in the last third of the nineteenth century. This painting shows Monet's son Jean at the table and the boy's mother, Camille, with her back to the window in a scene of informal family life.

Beside these reasons, I would like to suggest that two other developments pushed men into taking the domestic environment more seriously. The first, that the home created a place for men, has already been mentioned in Chapter 6. It offered them opportunities for participation beyond the fact that it was where they were the ultimate rulers and where they were serviced in order to carry out their more important life in the wider world. The ideology of family life that developed around the middle-class home was sold through magazines and books as a place of comfort, recreation and pleasure for all the family, including the man of the house and the children. This meant that while women may not have played much of a role in the professional lives of their husbands, except as powers behind the throne, men played an increasingly important part in the domestic lives of women, enjoying the children, celebrating birthdays and Christmas, and playing their part in hosting entertainments with their social equals.

The second was that as women's role within the home became more varied and more powerful, it became a place of fascination to men. Indeed, for some men, I think it held a status equal to the male world, something to be taken seriously in terms of a power base. Although men literally owned the home, women increased their power within it as the century developed. Bit by bit, the ideology evolved from theories of female moral authority to an acceptance of her growing economic and social powers. As the century progressed, the woman's role changed from angel in the house to something much more down to earth. One way that the chains binding women and home in the nineteenth century were both strengthened and made more tolerable was through the development of what has come to be called the consumer society. In the last third of the nineteenth century, female purchasing power increased dramatically, a development that boosted women's status in the home by expanding their role. The spending power of the middle-class female on herself, her home and her family meant that advertisements were aimed at her, magazines devoted to her and ever larger and more elaborate shops welcomed her. It is now over a hundred years since Thorstein Veblen in America argued in *The Theory of the Leisure Class* (1899) that

women displayed their husband's wealth and status through embellishing the home.

Their power was not just economic. Women's role within the home expanded during the nineteenth century. The restricted lives of most women of the higher classes (poor women had no choice but to try to earn a living) had always meant the home was their medium for self-expression. But after mid-century improved female education, women's increased involvement in furnishing and arranging the home and their control of the social rituals of entertaining meant that the domestic interior became her empire. For the fortunate, far from being a prison, the home became a setting for the increasing variety and richness of their lives. If they wanted to read the newspaper or smoke a cigarette in their morning room or boudoir they could. If they wanted to change the wallpaper of the drawing room, 'their' territory, they could. 'Don't mix with the upholsterer,' Kerr warned the male readers of *The Gentleman's House.*[2]

Until the freedoms of the late nineteenth century enabled women to eat in cafés, to shop in the new department stores, to go to a matinée or ride in an omnibus, the home was the setting for their social life. They did not go out to clubs as men did, but no one could stop them visiting friends or controlling the seating plan at dinner. A knowledge of etiquette and an understanding of the nuances of social life became a major way of bending the world to their needs. The male colleagues of Berthe Morisot were free to meet each other in the cafés of Paris in the 1870s. In order that her ambitious daughter would not be disadvantaged, Mme Morisot made sure that she invited these artists to her weekly at-homes so that her daughter could play a part in the cultural networks so important to professional success.

We hear so much about tyrant fathers and husbands that it is important to put the alternative view of the middle-class home as a female power base. Sometimes men were allowed to take a part. Sometimes they were excluded from its rituals and could only wonder. Despite their official control of the home in terms of finance and hierarchy, the fact that it was a female territory gave them an occasional sense of being unnecessary at certain female rituals or of having to defer to women's social machinations. As the woman's power within the home increased, I suspect that it began to seem more interesting to male eyes, a comparable place to the masculine world of work.

In fact, I would go further and speculate that for some artists, this new status of the woman in the home made the domestic interior exotic. I also think it made women more exciting or at least more interesting. It is well known that the male Impressionists were fascinated by the differences between male and female, particularly in the case of shop girls, laundresses or ballet girls of the lower classes. But I think the interest also extended upwards and the drawing rooms and boudoirs of the higher classes became irresistibly alluring to male artists, their own as well as other people's.

In 1865, Degas gave Manet a small painting he had made of him sprawling on a sofa listening to his wife playing the piano. Manet so disliked Degas' treatment of Suzanne Leenhoff's face that he cut off the edge of the painting, causing a temporary cooling of their friendship. In 1867–8, Manet painted his wife playing the piano in his mother's Paris apartment, where they were living at the time, a work that was fittingly, since his wife was Dutch, based on a seventeenth-century painting by Gabriel Metsu.

Even a committed *plein airiste* such as Monet painted interiors at a time when his family was overwhelmingly important to him. Between 1867 and 1875, when he was most involved in the passions and pleasures of family life, Monet painted several interiors showing his baby son Jean and Camille, the boy's mother. At the time of the earliest paintings, he wrote to his fellow-painter Frédéric Bazille about his happiness with his little family and his plans 'to do two figure paintings, an interior with a baby and two women',[3] an intention he carried out with *Dinner*, showing the baby, Camille, a female friend and a neighbour and *After Dinner* with Camille, a friend and a neighbour. Camille also posed at the window for *The Luncheon*, painted in 1868, and probably also for the woman at the table with Jean. In June 1870, Monet married Camille and a few months later the couple went to London so he could avoid the call-up for the Franco-Prussian War. Here he painted *Meditation: Madame*

Monet on a Sofa (1871), the most Whistlerian of his works with
its strong silhouette, geometric composition and the muted
tones of London light. In 1875, came *Apartment Interior*, an
unusual image of his home in Argenteuil with strong
compositional links to the contemporaneous *sous-bois*
images, in which Camille and Jean are almost incidental to
the light that streams in through the window and turns the
parquet floor to glass. It was bought by Caillebotte who was
interested in the bourgeois interior as a subject; almost half
of the works he showed at the Impressionist exhibitions were
set in successive family apartments.[4]

There is an oddness about Caillebotte's paintings that
contemporaries tried to deal with by relating his work to that
of realist novelists such as Zola. I think it is simpler than
that. Caillebotte's oddness comes from his depiction of men
in ways that had previously been reserved for women and his
depiction of women without their usual coat of femininity.

His men are often shown in the domestic interior, drying
themselves after a bath, sitting on sofas, looking out of
windows and eating in the dark family salon. At the 1876
Impressionist exhibition, he exhibited three paintings of
family life based in his mother's apartment, proof that the
relationship of men to the home had changed dramatically
and they could now be depicted in their domestic aspect.
Luncheon shows his mother and brother with the family butler
in attendance eating their elaborately laid lunch in the
gloomy dining room, with the artist's empty plate at the foot
of the painting. *Young Man Playing the Piano* shows his brother
Martial at the piano – an activity usually reserved in art to
display female posture and accomplishment – in a corner
of the salon wallpapered and carpeted in different floral
patterns. The third painting, *Young Man at his Window*, has
already been discussed (see p.60). This trio was light years
away from the traditional way of portraying men at a desk

Claude Monet
Apartment Interior, 1875

The composition of this extraordinary image with Camille in the shadows and Jean at the centre is closer to Monet's paintings of avenues of trees than to conventional presentations of the interior.

Gustave Caillebotte

Luncheon, 1876

Caillebotte's painting of a meal in his
mother's apartment shows his mother,
the servant and his brother René eating
lunch in bourgeois gloom and silence.
The empty plate in the foreground
stands in for the artist.

Gustave Caillebotte
Young Man Playing the Piano, 1876

Much of Caillebotte's output was based
on the successive family homes. Here,
he shows his brother Martial playing the
piano in the corner of the apartment at
rue de Miromesnil.

Opposite: **Gustave Caillebotte**
Portrait of a Man, 1877

Caillebotte did many paintings of men in domestic interiors. His intriguing treatment of what may be a portrait shrinks his sitter by aligning his head with the top of the sofa, an effect that is the opposite of masculine power.

Edouard Manet
Reading, 1868

Although in art the sofa is traditionally associated with women, as in Manet's exercise in filmy whites, after mid-century men appear on sofas, too, proof of the increasing importance of domestic life for men as well as women.

in a study or standing rock-like in a family portrait, the support of wife and children.

One of the ways that the domestic interior can be seen entering male minds as a suitable subject for their paintings is, curiously, through the depiction of the sofa. In art, the sofa is traditionally a female form of seating. Manet painted his wife enthroned on the sofa, her male companion excluded but allowed to lean his hand on the back. Berthe Morisot painted her mother and sister sitting side-by-side on a sofa, one contemplating her pregnancy, one reading a book. It is not that men never sat on sofas. Just that conventionally, particularly in portraiture but in genre paintings too, a hard chair or armchair were seen as appropriate for a man. But at some point after mid-century, the sofa became available to men as well as women – one more example of men bestowing notice and value on the

domestic interior because they now had a more comfortable place within it. The change can seem disturbing. The image of the male sitter in a corner of the sofa in Caillebotte's *Portrait of a Man* (1877) seems shocking because of the incongruity of the strict dark clothes against the patterned upholstery and the alignment of the top of his head with the back of the sofa, which results in making the man look miniaturized. The viewer is far more at home with Mme Manet's filmy white dress spread out upon the sofa.

The artists who put men in a domestic setting seem to be operating according to some unspoken rules. Although in the Impressionist years one finds men with women, men with servants or men with children, it is rare to find men pictured in groups. The literary scholar David Cecil famously pronounced in a lecture in Cambridge in 1935 that Jane Austen never wrote about two men together: 'She never describes a scene in which no woman is present; her heroes are shown to us, fragmentarily, and with character and motives in part unexplained, as they appeared to the girls with whom they came in contact.'[5] I would like to make a similar claim about domestic interiors, though not for the same reasons. Cecil believed that while Jane Austen could imagine the conversations of women or of men and women because she had experience of them, she did not feel qualified to reproduce the speech of men in their own company. Understandably, no women artists painted men together in a domestic situation, but more surprisingly, with some exceptions, neither did the men. Part of this reluctance was to do with the artistic conventions of representing men and women in painting. Apart from Caillebotte, who in 1881 painted a group of his friends playing cards in the apartment he shared with his brother Martial on the boulevard Haussmann, it was far more common to picture men together socially in studios or in clubs rather than in the home. Convention aside, the absence of men together in a home setting may be because both sexes still saw the domestic interior as a female space, a family space or a space for interaction between the sexes.

This may explain the tendency to feminize men when they do appear in a domestic context. When Vuillard paints

his brother-in-law, the artist Ker-Xavier Roussel, in 1903, he domesticates him into a father by showing him with his daughter and ensuring that everything about this interior exudes pleasure: the light, bright colour key of red and blue, the child's quaint sun bonnet, the contrasting patterns of the fabric and the father's relaxed, cross-legged pose with his back to the window. It is almost as if the decision to paint the male in a domestic interior requires him to be softened in some way.

Within a few years of its first exhibition in 1874, Impressionism became the most up-to-date style for young artists to adopt as they left art school, painting the world around them with the loose brushstrokes and absence of narrative that was then considered modern art. By the end of the 1870s, avant-garde critics justified the sketchy quality of Impressionism as *the* style for contemporary subjects. J.K. Huysmans wrote in his review of the 1879 Salon that the detailed finish of Flemish techniques, 'excellent for rendering the peaceful interiors in which good fat mothers smiled, are powerless to render the upholstered interiors of our day.'[6] Like all such quotes, it is wide open to the charge of special pleading and one can argue with it. But what is unarguable is the acceptance of the contemporary interior as a subject that needs no apology. While conservative artists were continuing with their stories and their histories, the fact that a high-profile group of artists, complete with vocal and heavyweight literary supporters, had given their blessing to a new informality of subject matter – an everyday life for the most part devoid of obvious moral or story – gave a lead for other artists to follow.

In the early 1880s, the young Belgian James Ensor, who has earned his place in the history of art for his macabre imagery of Christianity come down to earth, painted his family's bourgeois apartment, full of clutter and with dim light trying to force its way through heavily curtained windows. In 1881, aged twenty-one, he did two such paintings, *Ostende Afternoon* and *The Bourgeois Sitting Room*. Both show his mother and sister, but it is the atmosphere of these rooms in which you can hear the clock ticking as the women work or take their tea, that is the real subject. Though done around the same time, the *Oyster Eater*, for

which Ensor's sister posed in a corner of the apartment, is in a new and lighter key, and was exhibited in the 1883 exhibition of Les XX, the avant-garde group of which Ensor was a founding member. Further evidence that he was interested in rooms as a subject is *Girls Dressing* (1886), a painting resulting from his first visit to England. Oddly unrelated to other works he was doing at this period, two pubescent girls stand naked amid the grandeur of a room painted in a Turner-like yellow key.

Rooms of their own played an important role in the lives of the young women who made up the first wave of female art-school students. Many chose to study in Paris, which had an artistic culture ready to receive them, with classes for women, rooms to rent and, most important of all, a general acceptance that art was a suitable career for women. It is impossible to overestimate the importance of independence for these young women as for the first time in their lives, away from families and familiar surroundings, they established their own homes.

In 1900, the young Paula Modersohn-Becker wrote to her family that 'Monday I move to a little room that I'll furnish casually – like Mama's furniture made out of boxes. I won't have to lose my temper anymore with the waiter who hasn't made up my room by five in the afternoon. Now I'll fumble in my own room by myself.'[7] Ten days later she reported that all was running smoothly: 'My first piece of furniture (the first was my bed – so really my second) was a broom. Hand towels, dish towels and dust rags are already in effective operation.'[8]

These rooms were often shared with their easels and assorted artistic paraphernalia, as well as with other students, and they led to a new kind of domestic interior: the studio homes that signalled their independence and their professionalism. Recipients of a recognized training, aware of the new trends, mixing with male artists, they painted, as women had always done, their own domestic interior, but now it represented their artistic freedom rather than their second-class citizenship of the world of art. With love they painted the rooms in which they experienced the independence and camaraderie of their lives, sometimes empty, sometimes with signs of themselves, such as a palette or a painting, sometimes with friends and colleagues.

Edouard Vuillard
The Painter Ker-Xavier Roussel and his Daughter, 1903

The new importance of the entertainments and rituals of family life, and the development of the home as a welcoming place for both sexes, meant that the pleasures of domesticity became as important for men as for women at the end of the nineteenth century. No doubt unconsciously, Vuillard marks this change with this portrait of his brother-in-law relaxing with his daughter in an airy light-filled room.

Opposite: **James Ensor**

Ostende Afternoon, 1881

At the start of his career Ensor did
several works based on his mother's
apartment. The revolution brought
by Impressionism meant that all the
ingredients to make a painting were at
home – the light, the bourgeois clutter,
the afternoon refreshments in the
family salon.

James Ensor

The Oyster Eater, 1882

Ensor has moved into a lighter, brighter
key and a more expansive pictorial
vision in this painting, but the subject,
his sister at table, remains domestic and
close at hand.

Kitty Kielland
Studio Interior, Paris, 1883

This painting of the apartment Kielland
shared with fellow Norwegian Harriet
Backer spells out their artistic creed.
The landscape on the wall, the Japanese
fans and parasol and, above all, the
informality of the work itself, with its
cut-off furniture, pretty light and
absence of story, show their allegiance
to Impressionism.

The Norwegian painters Kitty Kielland and Harriet Backer went to study art in Paris and in *Studio Interior, Paris* (1883) Kielland painted Backer reading in their shared attic-studio in rue de l'Université, a document of their time as students. The Scandinavian women who studied in Paris were among the first to adopt the Impressionist agenda and the two artists' artistic allegiances are on display, from the Japanese fan through the concern with interior light effects to the Impressionist landscape on the wall. Kielland's inclusion of a corner of the portrait Backer was painting of her makes this a tribute to female friendship and shared goals at a time of artistic change. So much is made of the bohemian camaraderie of the young male students of the period, that it is good to have proof in this image of shared living space that women also had their fun, freedom and ambition.

Intimacy is an inevitable element of many of these paintings of the artists' own interiors. In 1890, the Danish artist P.S. Krøyer found the sight of his new wife at the easel in their room at Ravello in Italy an irresistible subject. In *Interior, Marie Krøyer Painting*, the light falling on her palette from the window, the filmy curtains and the airiness of the room convey the experience of the strong southern light that enchanted so many northerners. Little more than a sketch, it speaks of

love in an interior. The English Post-Impressionist Harold Gilman, who was part of Sickert's circle, paints his youngest sister Irene in the country rectory in Romney Marsh where his father was the vicar in *Edwardian Interior* (1900–5). Ethel Sands' light, bright *Woman at a Dressing Table* (1905–6) is thought to show her companion, the American painter Nan Hudson.

By the early twentieth century, a used and loved room, with people or without, is an accepted subject. Spencer Gore's *Interior: 31 Mornington Crescent* (1910), set in the communal sitting room of the house in northwest London where he was living at the time, sums up the change that had happened over the previous century. This was not just a new subject, but one that both painter and viewer had learned to appreciate and respond to.

Left: **P.S. Krøyer**
Interior, Marie Krøyer Painting, 1890

Krøyer paints his wife in a southern room full of light and love.

Below: **Spencer Gore**
Interior, 31 Mornington Crescent, 1910

The patterns, light and colour of Gore's home mark the coming of age of the interior.

Overleaf: **Ilya Repin**
Study of a Family Portrait, 1905

The activity in the Russian painter Repin's lively study is intimately allied to the domestic pleasures and occupations of the home.

9 coming of age

By the end of the nineteenth century, paintings of modest but entrancing interiors began to emerge with regularity from artists' studios. Even when they are inhabited, the people seem to play a part in the presentation of the room, instead of the other way around. The various developments that had taken place through the century – the empty room, light effects as a reason for art, the portrait that includes the sitter's surroundings, the genre paintings that site their social comments in the home, the artist's own home as a subject – came to fruition at its end. For the first time, domestic interiors had self-confidence. No longer hiding behind notions of portraiture or genre, these paintings emerge to form a new category of their own. What we are seeing is the triumph of the interior across all the divisions I have talked about.

There are dozens of artists in Europe and America whose work offers evidence of the interior's new importance. All countries were affected, from Russia, where Mariya Yakunchikova-Weber summoned the ghosts of enjoyable social gatherings in a painting of the protective covers swathing the chairs and chandeliers of the salon of her house, to Belgium, where Xavier Mellery dreamed of catching the soul of inanimate things in etchings and drawings of corners of his home, and Austria, where Carl Moll's *Interior* (1903) displayed a decor of Viennese art nouveau. It is hard to imagine before this period a work such as Harriet Backer's painting, *The Library of Thorvald Boeck* (1902), being considered for inclusion in a show of avant-garde art. But by 1900 a major change had taken place across the world of art and the manner of a painting outweighed concern with its content.

Although I have tried to chart the domestic interior's coming of age, it is impossible to be scientific about its development. Its evolution did not happen tidily. Propelled into art from all sorts of sources, everything fed into everything else, but none of it can be proved. Not all countries did the same thing, or if they did, they did not do it in the same decade. The inevitable time lag between the art worlds of the different countries meant that what one artist achieved by 1880 was reached by an artist of a different nationality in 1910 and of course it emerged with national characteristics.

I have explained its emergence in terms of social changes as they affected art and the century's drive to realism, which peaked with the Impressionist embrace of daily life. But there are other influences, too. Impressionism was the dominant movement of the last third of the century and most later nineteenth-century artists had an Impressionist phase prior to adopting the newer styles that followed it. But although Impressionism changed art for ever, not all the artists of the interior were Impressionists. With hindsight it can be seen that far from following the line of mainstream art history and being all Baudelaire, Impressionism and modern subject matter, the stylistic changes that were afoot entered art from all sorts of places, as two English art school lectures given several years apart, make clear. While the Impressionists in Paris were breaking rules with subjects drawn from the world around them and compositions inspired by the unusual angles of photography, the old beliefs were still being preached to students in academies all over the western world. In 1871,

Mariya Yakunchikova-Weber
Covers

Like many women at the end of the nineteenth century, Yakunchikova-Weber, a member of a wealthy cultured Russian family, trained in Paris. She believed that by studying her country, her house and her favourite corner of the garden, she could touch the universal and eternal.

Harriet Backer
The Library of Thorvald Boeck, 1902

Backer's debt to the Impressionism she was exposed to as a student in Paris is clear in the rich colours and glints of light of this interior. Interiors, particularly farm interiors of her native Norway, were among this artist's favourite subjects.

historical works made their name and fortune: 'The realism of modern art is due partly to a greater knowledge of, and a greater attention to costume, architecture, furniture, and all the properties of the stage on which we place our personages, but it is also due to our making truth a primary object.'[2] The word interior was not mentioned, but in discussing realism he showed his awareness of one of the changes that prepared the ground for the interior's entry into art. The conservative nineteenth-century taste for smoothly detailed painting was one influence on the trend to treat everything, even the humble domestic interior, with visual respect.

Another contributing factor to the coming of age of the domestic interior was that Dutch seventeenth-century genre paintings had one of their periodic surges of influence in the second half of the century, offering inspiration and prototypes to artists interested in light, the interior and modern life. They gave the Old Masterly seal of approval to the artists' current inclinations. We see this clearly in the large number of Scandinavian and German paintings of women in interiors, with doors framing vistas into other rooms, which update the seventeenth century by deleting the moralized story. Few artists were untouched. A surprising number of the new interiors by the most modern artists of their day, including Manet, Degas and Vuillard, had de Hooch or Maes behind them as a compositional influence and sometimes mood as well.

The flat shapes of Japanese prints nesting one into the other were a powerful inspiration to some, as was the art of Gauguin after 1890 for similar reasons of shape and colour. Whistler was a huge influence, on the Americans and British in particular, not so much his early works as the portraits from the 1870s of his mother and Carlyle, with their geometric flatness that linked back to the formal structure of Vermeer. The muted tonalities of the work of this artist who was claimed by three countries – America where he was born, England where he worked and lived the longest, and France where he was influential in the 1850s – were an inspiration to many painters who were not completely comfortable with Impressionist and Post-Impressionist colour and lack of structure. Whistler's horizontals and

the painter and professor Edward J. Poynter reiterated the conventional advice that surroundings should be 'only sufficient to add to the impressiveness of the scene and give such local character as may be deemed necessary.'[1] But a few years later, even academic teaching began to change. Edward Armitage, whose lectures on painting to Royal Academy students were published in 1883, acknowledged the realism in the works of the French artists Paul Delaroche and Jean-Léon Gérôme – two artists who are hardly cutting edge in the history of art, but whose minutely finished

Adolf Heinrich-Hansen

A Woman Reading in an Interior, 1918

After 1850 the quiet domestic scenes of the Dutch seventeenth-century little masters were increasingly admired. Few artists of the interior remained uninfluenced, particularly when it came to composition, but it was the Scandinavians above all who consciously continued the tradition.

influenced by the piles of material surrounding him in his dressmaker mother's home makes him a member of the select group of artists of the interior attracted to beautiful fabrics. Tissot, whose portraits include the most luxuriantly painted materials, was the son of a linen draper and a modiste, and much of his work can seem like a tribute to the glories of fabric and style. And in the early years of the twentieth century Matisse began to include in his paintings the favourite fabrics he carried from home to home.)

But Vuillard was not the only master of the interior at this time. He made these paintings as part of a group of artists called the Nabis (Hebrew for prophets), who through their graphic work for the theatre, in particular the realistic

Pierre Bonnard
The Meal, 1899

The vast white tabletop suggests the child's perspective as well as the vast gulf between youth and age.

Pierre Bonnard
Man and Woman, 1900

The enclosed quality of Bonnard's interior suggests the world of private sexual pleasures.

verticals related to the new concept of the canvas as a field for the artist's pattern but without the open-endedness of Impressionist compositional ideas, while his rejection of narrative echoed the latest thinking from France. There were influences from literature as well, particularly from the realism of modern writers such Zola and Strindberg and their stress on the tensions of family life.

It was now, at the end of the century, that a new phenomenon appeared: the artist who specialized in interiors. The great name known to all is Vuillard, who in his miraculous decade from 1894 to 1904 produced an unprecedented series of interiors in which a dazzle of colour and pattern slowly resolves into descriptions of furniture, fabric and people as neatly interlocked as a completed jigsaw. The surface complexity of Vuillard's images of female lives passed in sedentary activity indoors rivals the Japanese printmakers he revered. (The often-repeated suggestion that Vuillard's patterned pictures were drama coming out of Scandinavia, were aware of the issues surrounding contemporary domestic life. When the interior is discussed, Vuillard may be the best-known member of the group, but around 1900 Bonnard and Vallotton painted a number of paintings that are very close in style to his.

Our view of Bonnard's work is dominated by his early Japanese-influenced prints and paintings of Parisian street life and later by the decades of spectacular canvases he produced of his partner Marthe de Méligny going about her domestic and personal duties. The explosive colouring of these paintings and their dazzling light, which seems to spring out from the canvas like a backlit transparency, tend to hide the fact that in the 1890s Bonnard painted some equally wonderful but lower-keyed interiors which share some characteristics with the works of Vuillard.

Bonnard, like Vuillard and Vallotton, worked from his home in his early days and, also like the other two, based many paintings on the interiors of his bourgeois family. Several are set in his childhood home at Le Clos, presided over by his grandmother Mme Frédéric Mertzdorff. *The Meal* of 1899 shows his niece Renée Terrasse at table with her great-grandmother, a strange image showing each immersed in her own world and one that suggests a child's-eye view with its huge expanse of tablecloth. He painted Renée again in the same year, this time with her two brothers and her mother, Bonnard's sister. *Young Woman by Lamplight*, painted around 1900, shows how close he was to the style of Vuillard at this period.

These intimate family scenes were not the only type of interior that concerned him. When Marthe comes into his life, the paintings become more personal and the scene changes from shared family room to the private world of the bedroom. The sexual honesty of several of Bonnard's works at this time, such as *Indolente* (*c.*1899), a portrait of Marthe sprawled on the bed, reveals how a world can be created from domestic sexual pleasures. The mutual sexual discovery that marks the double portrait *Man and Woman* of 1900, in which Bonnard shows himself about to get dressed after the act of making love, uses the routine domesticity of the bedroom to make the same point.

The link between sexual intimacy and the artist's own interior is particularly strong in Bonnard – in fact I think he is the master of this particular subject. I suspect that for a painter such as Bonnard, drawn to the private world of a woman, a studio setting would have had all the appeal of the

Pierre Bonnard
The Bathroom Mirror, 1908

Bonnard emphasizes the voyeurism of this scene by showing the women reflected in the mirror.

Opposite left: **Félix Vallotton**
The Top Hat, 1887

The top hat on the chair and the
suggestively open door brings this little
room to life.

Opposite right: **Félix Vallotton**
Woman Searching Through a Cupboard, 1900

This brilliant image displays Vallotton's
sensitivity to the drama of artificial light,
an effect he explored in several paintings
at this time.

artificial habitat of a zoo. In *The Bathroom Mirror* of 1908, his voyeurism is made explicit as he looks at the model through a mirror. It is not a world for men and to make sure we understand that, he paints a second woman with a teacup sharing in this secret society of female rituals.

The interiors that the third member of the trio, the Swiss Félix Vallotton, painted for no more than a decade are unlike any others. Even before he had absorbed the modern plays examining the troubled family unit, the colour of Gauguin and the pattern and flatness of the Japanese print, he had shown an interest in the dramatic possibilities of rooms. The Dutch-influenced *Top Hat* of 1887, painted when he was twenty-two, is little more than an open door, a chair and table, but what catches our eye is the top hat on the chair. Vallotton understands the potential of a room in the way that poets do: not much is needed to set a scene that liberates the imagination. Setting a scene is exactly the impression of a painting five years later, *The Sick Woman*, an oddly appealing little work whose composition brings to mind a weather clock where Mr Rain goes in as Mrs Sun comes out. As in *The Top Hat*, Vallotton brings us right into the action, in this case by seating us in the front row of the stalls where we can watch the mistress and the maid. In *Woman Doing her Hair* of 1900, his wife sits to one side at the

Félix Vallotton
Woman Doing her Hair, 1900

A classic scene of domesticity in which
the real subject is the colour and the bold
shapes of the objects.

dressing table but the real subject is the room and the crisp
shapes and patterns it frames.

Vallotton's fascination with the illuminated domestic
interior led to a handful of unusual paintings. He
made lamplight the focal point in *The Visit* of *c.*1897, a
disconcerting painting that is as much a portrait of two
lampshades as of the shadowy women who meet in the
murk. Instead of presenting the interior in a detailed
and informative manner, he uses distortions of scale and
dramatic light effects to conjure up an image of a room
at night. The startling *Woman Searching Through a Cupboard*
(1900), despite its fashionable homage to the strong
outlines and vertical format of the Japanese print, is the
work of someone entranced by the visual delights of life
in the home and who has the compositional ability to
make the most of them.

It was in these years that Matisse's fascination with the interior emerged. He was one of those artists who went through a range of styles at the start of his career and he took some time to settle on his subject of the woman in an interior. At the beginning, the interiors are merely one among many other subjects, with few features of their later face. In 1895, he painted *Woman Reading*, a subject that had become conventional by the 1880s. It is a quiet and rather sombre painting, though the flash of green in the jug on the mantelpiece points to the mastery of colour that he later made his own. *Girl Reading*, from 1905, displays a much brighter palette and Matisse is less concerned with a realistic treatment, in keeping with his modernist concerns. It is the start of the painter's obsession with the female figure in a room.

In Scandinavia, interiors were a popular subject among artists. There was even a favourite format, involving a woman at her domestic duties, traceable back to seventeenth-century Holland. Denmark in particular produced a number of artists who specialized in the subject. Anna Ancher was the one Danish Impressionist to return to the interior throughout her life. *Sunshine in the Blue Room* (1891) is a study in blue and yellow of a golden-haired child in which everything is peace and pleasure. Her hair, her reel of cotton and the shadow of the plant owe their existence to the light that floods into the room. In 1918, Ancher painted an interior of her parents' hotel on Skagen, the artists' colony where she met her artist husband Michael when he came to paint there at the end of the 1870s. She produced many more interiors in between, together with the genre scenes and portraits that also interested her.

Hammershøi produced more than sixty interiors between 1888 and 1914. His life-long passion for the mystery of the rooms he lived in makes him Vuillard's rival as master of the painted interior, though their styles are very different. Unlike Vuillard, Hammershøi is an artist of line and

Carl Holsøe
In the Dining Room

Although influenced by the calm geometry of Hammershøi, Holsøe was also drawn to the details of daily life. This exploration of the effect of candlelight on glass and china looks back to the art of seventeenth-century Holland.

Carl Holsøe
An Interior with a Cello

By 1900, a pleasant interior vista was sufficient subject matter for a painting. No story was necessary, although the cello signifies the human – maybe female – presence.

atmosphere not brushstroke and colour: 'What makes me select a motif is just as much the lines in it, what I would call the architectonic attitude in the picture', he said in an interview in 1907. 'And then the light, naturally….Of course the colour is not immaterial…I work much on making it harmonic. But when I select a motif, I think that first and foremost it is the lines I look at.'[3] He talked about the first interior he did in 1888: 'I have always thought there was such beauty about a room like that, even though there weren't any people in it, perhaps precisely when there weren't any.'[4] His work has something of the quality of Vermeer, in the way he turns the furnishings into geometry and in his gift for atmosphere. The women he occasionally includes are as uninflected as the chairs they sit on. Often he paints their back view, making them a human shape among the furniture shapes of his sombre colour palette. Hammershøi's heightened sensitivity to the light and atmosphere of rooms gives his work a kind of hyper-reality that did not emerge again until the Surrealists' attempts to replicate their dreams in paint and the clock-stopped interiors of Edward Hopper.

Hammershøi created his own little circle of influence. His friend Carl Holsøe's fondness for the empty room and the lone woman seen from the back are taken from the master, although little of Hammershøi's reductive tendency survives Holsøe's more conventional realism. Slightly closer to Hammershøi's atmospheric spirit was his brother-in-law

Opposite: **Peter Ilsted**
The Artist's Daughters in an Interior at Liselund

Ilsted uses his daughters to enliven the pared-down ovals and squares of the furniture, which owe much to the vision of his brother-in-law Hammershøi.

Peter Ilsted. The frontal geometry of his works echoes Hammershøi's images, although his treatment of the figures is more realistic. *Interior with a Young Girl Serving Tea* (1901) exemplifies these similarities and differences most clearly. *The Artist's Daughters in an Interior at Liselund* is a classic example of the new type of domestic interior in the way it manages to combine an uninflected visual description of interior space with just enough detail to hold the viewer's interest.

The interior was an important subject for Norway's Harriet Backer and she returned to it throughout her life.

There is no hidden story in her *Blue Interior* of 1883, just a desire to create a sense of beauty by painting the room as a harmony in complementary colours. *Chez Moi* (1887), depicts a young woman, perhaps herself, at the piano, her sheet music catching the last light from the window. *My Studio* (1918), is a painting of the security of her work space. Like Cassatt and Morisot before her, Backer endows female activities with dignity. *By Lamplight* (1890), lets us into a room of a young girl studying late into the night as the lamplight makes strange shadows on the walls.

Harriet Backer
By Lamplight, 1890

A modern version of Kersting's lamplit scenes from the start of the century, Backer, like so many women artists of the period, paints a studious young girl, as if to claim seriousness for her sex.

In America, Edmund C. Tarbell earned a reputation for his paintings of women in interiors. These are subject paintings, posed in a carefully arranged studio space, but they are also paintings of an artist who wants to convey the beauty of interior light. The viewer of *Across the Room* (*c.*1899) (see p.9) sees the relaxed, seated woman across a great expanse of polished floor, which is transfigured by the light streaming in through the window. In *The Breakfast Room* (*c.*1903), he reverses this relationship by placing the figures in the foreground with a gleaming expanse of floor and a door through to another room in the background. The modish glamour of these images is influenced by Impressionist compositional formats and brushstrokes, the tonality of Whistler and the dash of Sargent's portraits.

Around 1905, Tarbell's interiors took a softer turn and began to carry a set of values with immense appeal to the public. Their surface display of peace and poetry is built on the influence of the Dutch masters of the interior. Paintings such as *Girls Reading* (*c.*1906–7), *New England Interior* (*c.*1907) and *Young Girl Studying* (1914) are full of what were perceived as the New England values of simplicity and hard work. Links were made between the grave young women (often the artist's daughters) absorbed in their reading or sewing and the simple interiors (deceptively simple since they were based on his own home, which happened to be full of desirable furniture and ceramics). The comforting picture of domestically employed young womanhood came at a time – disturbing for some – when women were becoming independent members of the workforce. The artist named one of these interiors, *Girl Mending* (*c.*1910), as one of his two best pictures. When asked why, he replied that 'I think I have come nearer to making the atmosphere of the actual scene before me than I ever did before,' which seems to me a clinching argument that other qualities besides subject matter had become increasingly important.[5] Far from a mere reworking of genre, which is how some critics categorized Tarbell, this is the domestic interior invested with specific powers of its own.

The British, too, produced their specialists in interiors at this time. The earliest examples were done by the brothers-in-law William Rothenstein and William Orpen, who used

Edmund C. Tarbell
*The Breakfast Room, c.*1903

Tarbell's off-centre composition, which owes much to Impressionism, makes the shining floor, the screen and the door the focus of this image.

Edmund C. Tarbell
*Girl Mending, c.*1910

Tarbell felt that he had caught the atmosphere of this corner of his home with great success. It is heavily influenced by the works of Whistler.

William Orpen
A Window in a London Street, 1901

In England around 1900, Orpen and William Rothenstein developed their ideas about painting interiors. This is based on a room in London's Fitzrovia.

William Rothenstein
Hampstead Interior, 1903

In this bold composition the young Rothenstein places more emphasis on the room than on the woman.

their young wives, the beautiful Knewstub sisters, as their models. In the beginning, it seems to have been a family affair, emerging out of excited discussions between the young marrieds. In 1900, William Rothenstein painted his wife and sister-in-law in *The Browning Readers* (see p.7), perhaps inspired by his recent portrait of the founder of the Browning Society, an organization devoted to the work of the poet who had many followers at this period. In 1901, came Orpen's *A Window in a London Street*, a woman gazing out of a huge window onto a street in Fitzrovia, one of the London quarters favoured by artists, and Rothenstein's *Hampstead Interior*, a woman moving aside the curtain as she looks out of a room composed in neat Whistlerian horizontals.

Around the middle of the decade Orpen painted a group of striking interiors based on a window in his home in Chelsea. *Night (no.2)*, painted in 1907, is a scene of passionate intimacy, showing Orpen's wife bending back her head to receive her husband's kiss. Done in the early years of his marriage, when his studio was in his home, this group of paintings looks as new within the British painting tradition as the work of the avant-garde artists across the Channel.

Orpen and Rothenstein exhibited at the New English Art Club, the self-consciously modern alternative to the Royal Academy, and between 1905 and 1910 they were joined by others who flirted with the idea of the interior, including Lavery, the husband and wife Ambrose and Mary McEvoy and George Clausen, whose stunning *Twilight, Interior (Reading by Lamplight)* was painted in about 1909, the year after he became a Royal Academician.

The art world recognized that something new was happening and attempted to pin down the origins of the trend. Rothenstein himself had no doubts, giving 1900 as the date: 'On our return to London, I began to work on some small "interior" subjects.'[6] And 'Thus for a time, Orpen's pictures were confused with mine; indeed I think Orpen would have agreed that at this period he was somewhat influenced by my "interiors".'[7] His use of the inverted commas round the word interiors suggests its novelty.

William Orpen
Night (no.2), 1907

The mood of this painting is created by the black night outside the window, establishing the room as a haven of privacy.

George Clausen

Twilight, Interior (Reading by Lamplight),
*c.*1909

This painting, which evokes the warmth
and cosiness that is the special quality
of the illuminated room at night,
Clausen shows himself affected by
the fashion for interiors among his
fellow London artists.

Most commentators agreed and named Rothenstein's *The Doll's House* of 1899–1900 as the first example of the subject. The artist Augustus John, who modelled for the standing man, said in an interview in the 1950s that it was based on Ibsen's play and Rothenstein recalled the setting as the quirky staircase of a house he and his wife had rented at Vattetot in Normandy in the summer of 1900 where they were the centre of a group of artists including John, the Australian Charles Conder, Orpen and Rothenstein's brother Albert: 'At Yport, two miles away, lived a tailor, who sold corduroy and a coarse blue linen, such as the fishermen wear in those parts. The corduroy took John's fancy, and he presently appeared, a superb figure, in a tight jacket and wide pegtop trousers; so superb that I painted him standing beside my wife, my wife sitting on the staircase I mentioned earlier.'[8]

Another sign of recognition was the fact that these works were illustrated in the art magazines, indicating their acceptability as well as their novelty. Rothenstein's *Interior* was illustrated in the *Art Journal* in 1901, Orpen's *Night* in 1908 in the *Magazine of Art*. And there were comments as well as pictures. A review of an exhibition at the New English Art Club in the 1908 *Art Journal* reported that 'Professor Fred Brown, Mr Muirhead, Mr Walter Sickert, Mrs McEvoy express their individual art in studies of interiors.'[9] In a review in 1909, the *Studio* declared: 'The paintings of interior genre in the present exhibition were unusually numerous, indicating quite a movement in this direction.'[10]

The readers of the *Art Journal* were left in no doubt that the interior was also being painted in other countries. 'The continental artists included M. Blanche in a brilliant but unharmonized interior, all in blue, M. Bussy, whose clever lamp-lit interior asserted itself beside the subtler *Night* of Mr Orpen, M. Le Sidaner, M. Aman-Jean and M. Besnard.'[11] Besides the three English works illustrating an article in the *Studio* on the subject in 1909, there were two paintings by Hammershøi, three by Jacques-Emile Blanche and one by Félix Bracquemond, the husband of the Impressionist Marie Bracquemond.[12]

The mystery is that despite contemporary recognition, it would be nearly one hundred years before the domestic interior entered art history as a recognized category. It is only recently that essays have taken to dealing with the subject.[13] Though I am using Britain as a case study, similar recognition and then silence happened in other countries, too. Hammershøi's obsessive interest is a relatively recent rediscovery and despite the success of Tarbell, the interior is not mentioned in most histories of American art.

Although contemporary commentators could see something new was entering art, they had trouble analysing what it was. I think there were two reasons for this. The first was the unwillingness of many artists to drop the story, despite their awareness that narrative was waning in the face of a new concentration on style and composition. Sickert argued with overstatement but some perception that 'The New English Art Club picture has tended to be a composite product in which an educated colour vision has been applied to themes already long approved and accepted in this country.'[14] There is a lot of truth to this. Both *The Doll's House* and *The Browning Readers* hint at a subject, even if it was treated without the mid-Victorian scattering of clues. Even an artist as committed to the interior as Orpen seems loathe to jettison narrative completely. In 1905, he painted what amounted to a double of the 1901 *Window on a London Street*, which he called *The Refugees*. Same room, but the single woman looking out of the window has been replaced by a nervous family sheltering from some unnamed terror.

But I think the main reason why the emergence of the interior was overlooked is the way the critics tried to make sense of it. Reviews of the big art shows of the day followed a formula of dealing with the paintings under the traditional categories of portraiture, landscape and genre. Although the critics recognized the novelty of the interiors, when it came to writing the review, they dealt with them in the genre category, usually near the end of the piece (though always before the paragraph on the female exhibitors). The appearance of the new interiors was noted, but as part of the modern-life aspect of genre painting. A review of the New Salon in Paris in 1901 in the *Magazine of Art* explained: 'in all the various genres one single ruling idea seems to animate our artists, namely, that of presenting modern life, whether in landscape, portraiture or interiors.'[15] By anchoring the new interiors in genre painting, the critics

William Rothenstein

The Doll's House, 1899–1900

Rothenstein believed he originated the
interior as a subject. This is the earliest
example, and while somewhat theatrical,
it shows the young artist downplaying
the narrative in favour of atmosphere.

helped camouflage their emergence as a subject in its own right. This tendency to explain the interior in terms of genre painting almost – but not totally – made it invisible.

In one country alone they saw what was happening. In France, the novelty of the work of Vuillard above all but also of Vallotton and Bonnard in the last decade of the nineteenth century was recognized and put the interior on the art-history map. Only it was not called the domestic interior, it was called *intimisme*. These artists' complex but enchanting images of their family and friends conversing in living rooms or eating round the dining table, their new and claustrophobic feel, and the patterns made from their shapes, ensured that they were noticed and their character named. As early as 1892, a critic used the term *intimiste*: 'Mr Vuillard's scenes, his *Reclining Woman*, his *Women Mending*, his *Luncheon* prove him to be, once again, an *intimiste* with a delicious sense of humour.'[16] As in every other country, these new images of the interior were given an artistic provenance. But though Vallotton and Vuillard especially were linked to the genre paintings of the seventeenth-century Dutch artists this still did not prevent the French critics from seeing that something new had entered art.

It is with *intimisme* that we finally find official recognition and a definition of what was happening in the years around 1900. The *Dictionary of Art* mentioned in Chapter 2, which has no term for the interior, does have an entry for *intimisme*: 'Term applied to paintings depicting everyday life in domestic interiors, usually referring to the work of Pierre Bonnard and Edouard Vuillard. It was first used in the 1890s, although the type of paintings to which it refers had been produced earlier by such artists as Johannes Vermeer and Jean-Siméon Chardin.' As a term it was picked up internationally because everything that happened in France around 1900 is seen as important in the history of art, whereas what happened elsewhere is not always given such value.

And that is the problem. The exclusively French face of *intimisme* has ensured that the international development of the domestic interior as a genre has remained a secret. The fact that *intimisme* describes what happened in France in the art of Vuillard and Bonnard disqualifies it from speaking for all the other types of interiors that entered western art

around 1900. Though they appear at the same time, which suggests they deserve note as other aspects of the same movement, they do not match the *intimiste* criteria created to classify the paintings of Bonnard and Vuillard. The glory of the painting of Vuillard in particular, and the unquestioning acceptance that the movement he inspired is all there is to say about the matter, has blinded us to the bigger picture. These other interiors are victims of the *intimiste* label.

The second problem with the unquestioning acceptance of the label is that the artists who inspired it are stuck with it forever, even though in the twentieth century Vuillard broadened his style into portraiture and Bonnard opened his interiors to daylight and colour.

The third, more serious, problem with the *intimiste* label is that it cuts off further exploration. *Intimisme* as practised by Vuillard and Bonnard at the end of the nineteenth century was born of a marriage between the interest in brushstrokes, light and everyday subject matter of Impressionism and the fascination with pattern and two dimensions of Japanese prints and Gauguin's paintings. It is a tribute to its novelty that it was recognized as early as 1892. Vuillard, Bonnard, and a painting or two by Vallotton if he is lucky enough to be remembered, are labelled as *intimiste*, cutting off any more detailed discussion. But as we have seen, there were other factors inspiring other artists, or even the same factors inspiring them in different ways, resulting in interiors for which the label *intimisme* is an unhelpful, even impotent, description for what the painters were doing. The conventional way of seeing the art of the past has caused all other artists of the time to be measured against the achievements of Vuillard, Bonnard and Vallotton. The effect has been that all those artists who were attracted to the domestic interior, but handled it with a different sensibility, have been ignored, or called conventional or less artistically adventurous.

All the artists mentioned in this chapter were visual poets of the interior. Bonnard put it into words, talking about the poetry of the things he knew best, but it is obvious that others felt it too.[17] Three hundred years after landscape managed to break out of the background, the interior finally managed it too, even though it was signalled only by the sound of the French horn and not the full orchestra it deserved.

Maurice Lobre
Jacques-Emile Blanche's Cabinet de Toilette, 1888

Jacques-Emile Blanche was a successful and sociable French painter and this room-portrait is probably of his house on the outskirts of Dieppe. While Sickert was attracted to France, his friend Blanche was drawn to England where he exhibited yearly and had several patrons. On one of his trips he probably acquired the Morris and Co. chair standing by the washstand.

10   what happened next?

W hat happened next was that the domestic interior faded away. It was replaced by disdain for subject matter and the religion of colour, shapes and two-dimensional space that marked the avant-garde art of the new century.

What happened next was that the interior survived. Despite the advent of the 'isms' of modern art, many of which forced subject matter to take second place to the Holy Trinity of form, colour and the picture plane, the interior kept on going. It found a place in the realistic paintings of artists content to create pleasant images for a public bewildered or disgusted by the productions of the avant-garde, and it occasionally and surprisingly leapt into the public eye through an avant-garde movement such as Surrealism.

Two versions of events: the first is the conventional art-history one, with which I disagree, and the second is what actually happened.

The official story is that throughout the twentieth century domesticity was seen as the enemy of avant-garde art. In 1996, in his introduction to *Not at Home: The Suppression of Domesticity in Modern Art and Architecture*, a title which says it all, Christopher Reed describes how 'the domestic was the antithesis of art' for the influential American critics Clement Greenberg and Harold Rosenberg who set the art world's critical agenda after World War II. 'One of Greenberg's best-known essays,' he writes, 'defines the avant-garde through its opposition to "kitsch", a term identified with the knick-knacks of the middle class home….Imputations of domesticity could be inherently damning, as when

Greenberg attributed to some of Motherwell's paintings "an archness like that of the interior decorator who stakes everything on a happy placing".'[1] And yet, eight years after he edited this book of essays, Reed wrote *Bloomsbury Rooms: Modernism, Subculture, and Domesticity*, an investigation of the importance to that group of twentieth-century English artists of the rooms they not only lived in but made into art in several ways. One way was the brainchild of the prominent critic Roger Fry who set up the Omega Workshops in 1913 in an experiment to bring fine artists and domestic furniture together. Several members of the group painted screens and bowls and designed fabrics for the company. Another way was by decorating their own homes, sometimes, as was the case at Ham Spray, the house Dora Carrington shared with Lytton Strachey, in a fashion limited to a few pieces; other times, covering everything – furniture, walls, woodwork, fireplace surrounds – as was the case at Charleston, the Sussex farmhouse where the artists Vanessa Bell and Duncan Grant lived. The portrait Duncan Grant did of Vanessa Bell around 1916–17 reveals as much about the couple's artistic creed as it does about her as she sits in a room decorated with recognizable Omega objects.

Obviously, the interior did not fade from twentieth-century art. Aside from the Bloomsbury group's special skill of creating artistic backgrounds to their lives through the embellishments they made to their homes (strictly aesthetic it should be said; at first there was no central heating and only an earth closet at Charleston to serve the family, friends and lovers who congregated there), many artists continued to use the interior as a subject for their art. There is a spread

Duncan Grant
*Vanessa Bell, c.*1916–17

The Bloomsbury Group believed in applying art to life. Grant, who had just begun to live with the painter Vanessa Bell, places her in a room at Charleston, surrounded by fabrics and and pots from the Omega Workshops, which had been founded by their friend Roger Fry in 1913.

of wonderful interiors in the twentieth century, many of them influenced by the paintings done around 1900. John Wonnacott's placing in 2000 of the Royal Family, all animation and corgi dogs, at the centre of a palatial room of golden grandeur is surely a descendent of the vast interior of Lavery's royal portrait of 1913.

Throughout this book we have seen how the new subject and its assorted treatments introduced in the nineteenth century continued into the twentieth. Vilhelm Hammershøi and Walter Gay continued painting rooms until their deaths in 1916 and 1937 respectively. Gabriele Münter returned to the interior in the years approaching the First World War. Harold Gilman continued to make portraits of the rooms he lived in until his death in 1919. The human scale of the corner of his room with its friendly objects, modest paintings and light falling on the carpet from an open door is one of a series he did around 1914 and 1915. The room in *Tea in the Bed Sitter* (1916) is as much the subject of the painting as the women, and it also provides the chance to observe a social development, an agreeable offshoot of looking at paintings. These are nice women, perhaps teachers or typewriters, as they were called in a noun that sadly never caught on, able to live with a freedom unknown to middle-class women a century earlier and even, we might assume, enjoying in friendship a substitute for family life.

In Chapter 6, we saw how Lavery combined his early interest in interior spaces with his later portrait commissions. When, in 1908, a year after *Night (no.2)*, Orpen painted the wealthy American, Mrs St George, who it is thought became his mistress around this time, he posed her in her bedroom with a four-poster in the background.[2] Has he deliberately centred the bed like a baldachino in a religious Renaissance painting while the sitter stretches provocatively like a fallen angel at its feet?

Others did not just keep up their interest in interiors but continued to develop it well into the twentieth century. Bonnard went on for decades painting rooms, dinner tables, views through windows, his wife in the bathroom, in the bedroom, in the living room, but in a far brighter and more expansive manner than in his early works. The mature work of Bonnard reveals the limited power of the *intimiste* label of

John Wonnacott

The Royal Family: A Centenary Portrait, 2000

The artist plays off the sitters' informality against the interior grandeur of Buckingham Palace in this engaging portrait of four generations of the British Royal Family.

Harold Gilman

Tea in the Bedsitter, 1916

With his respectful treatment of the sparse but fresh interior, Gilman conveys the pleasures of independence for the young working women.

the 1890s – it cannot cope with the later shimmering images of his wife involved in the intimate female rituals of bathing, dressing or just dreaming. Although there is a voyeuristic feeling to some of these works, related to Degas' pastels of women washing themselves, they also have an expansive quality of their own, not just in terms of their size, which is often large, but in terms of their generous and lavish treatment. They transport the spectator to a world incandescent with light and colour conjured up by an artist deeply affected by the beauty of light in rooms. These great paintings of a figure in an interior, in which the tiles, the water and the woman herself are subsumed into colour and light, are responsible for thousands of imitators today.

In the early twentieth century, Vuillard lost his heightened vision and settled into being a painter of portraits in interiors. Although these are often rushed past with an embarrassed smile by admirers of his early works, they offer an insight into his struggle to balance the demands of sitter and surroundings, a struggle he did not have to face when his subject came from the non-paying, non-commissioning circle of friends and family. He clearly had mixed feelings about giving the portraits the upper hand, claiming that he was not a portrait painter: 'I don't paint portraits. I paint people in their home.'[3] Sometimes the interior seems to overwhelm the sitter, as in the portrait of Mme Fernand Javal of 1931, the wife of the owner of Houbigant Perfumes, and sometimes he gets the balance right, as in his portrait of Marie-Blanche de Polignac of 1928–32. He may have lost his youthful vision, but he never lost his love for colour, pattern and the feminine, setting many paintings in the bedroom, a reference perhaps to the eighteenth-century French tradition of receiving one's visitors while dressing for the day.

Impressionism has never died and to this day a woman in an interior remains one of the choices an artist can make from the library of styles and subjects. Sometimes clothed, sometimes not, nearly always in a sunlit room formed of bright colours and dashing brushstrokes, she has become a stock subject for painters everywhere, whether they display their work in academies, expensive galleries or on park railings. The subject is so popular that random examples

Opposite: **William Orpen**
Interior at Clonsilla with Mrs St George, 1908

In this portrait of a wealthy American
in her bedroom, Orpen has given an
extraordinary prominence to the four-
poster bed. The couple are thought to
have become lovers around this time.

Edouard Vuillard
Countess Marie-Blanche de Polignac, 1928–32

In the twentieth century, the *intimiste*
Vuillard became a celebrated portraitist,
although sometimes it seems his sitters
have to fight for attention with the
interiors with which he had made his
name at the end of the previous century.

Bessie Davidson
*Madame Le Roy Seated in an Interior, c.*1920

Davidson was part of the wave of
Australians who came to study art in
Europe in the early twentieth century.
The subject and style of this painting,
which has now become very established,
depicts a friend reading in Davidson's
Montparnasse apartment.

can be taken from any place and any time in the last one hundred years. Men as well as women paint this subject, but the differences first seen in the nineteenth century were still valid in the twentieth. Men chose it for artistic reasons, whereas for women it could express a social reality. Bessie Davidson lived in a world with a strong female presence. She had studied in Munich and Paris with her teacher, fellow-Australian Margaret Preston, and shared a studio with her on their return to Adelaide. She settled in a Montparnasse apartment in 1910 when she was thirty-one, and ten years later painted her friend Mme Le Roy reading there, in acknowledgement of their friendship.

But the twentieth-century interior is not confined to conservative painters. One of its greatest interpreters is Matisse, who by the end of the century's first decade was producing icons of modern art based on rooms treated as the raw material for ever more inventive combinations of pattern, line and colour. *The Red Studio* of 1911, a domestic-studio hybrid, is an incredibly bold composition in which he places skeletal yellow furniture and a postage-stamp-size selection of his work on a red ground. On the one hand, it has all the characteristics of the interior, with its positive mood and suggested human presence, yet on the other, this painting from the heroic days of modernism is all about technique and style, a manifesto painting in which the artist makes visible his beliefs about art. Attempts to explain the magic of *The Painter's Family* of the same year draw on comparisons with collage and patchwork but overall it is a breathtaking painting made by an artist who found in the interior all he could want in the way of inspiration.

Many Surrealists found rooms a fruitful source of imagery. They took a subject celebrated in art for its peace and predictability and distorted it to suggest displacement, unease and uncomfortable dreams. Magritte loved to play games with rooms, filling one with an oversize apple, changing the scale of another. Perhaps it is not surprising that an artist who liked to present himself in a bourgeois persona, complete with suit, tie and bowler hat, would understand the creative possibilities of subverting the icon of convention that was the domestic interior. In *Forbidden Reproduction* of 1937, a back view of Edward James looking

Henri Matisse
The Red Studio, 1911

Matisse here takes the interior, a favourite subject, and develops it into what is now recognized as a landmark painting of modern art.

in a mirror which in turn reflects his back view, he has the last word on the mirror. In *La Lunette d'Approche* of 1963, which he described in a letter as 'the window half opening on to absence of light', he takes the ideas of interior/exterior to a Surrealist conclusion of logical illogicality.[4] In *Eine Kleine Nachtmusik* of 1943, Dorothea Tanning, the American Surrealist and wife of Max Ernst, transforms a corridor into an uneasy dream by adding a giant sunflower on the red carpet, a door ajar onto a mysterious orange light and two young girls, one in a dream, the other with strangely levitating hair.

With the Kitchen Sink school of 1950s Britain, the interior gave its name to a type of painting dedicated to a realistic depiction of daily domesticity. John Bratby matched his unglamorous postwar living quarters with lumpy paint and strong brushstrokes. In France in 1952, Jean Hélion painted *Nude with Loaves*, showing the back view of an unidealized woman, a pair of trousers on a hook on the cracked wall and a boot beneath a table on which lie two long loaves of bread. Superficially related to the school of British postwar realism, it also vibrates with some unspoken message. Perhaps the room, the food and the sex refer to the basic needs of life.

It was inevitable that their fascination with the objects of contemporary life would lead Pop Artists to the interior. An iconic work of British Pop, *Just what is it that makes today's homes so different, so appealing?*, assembles a collection of consumer desirables within a living room. Richard Hamilton, who painted it in 1956, has returned at intervals to the interior as a subject of his art. Patrick Caulfield frequently explored his fascination with the tension between the flatness of the canvas and the three-dimensionality of real objects through the depiction of interiors. In the 1990s, the American Roy Lichtenstein did a series of huge canvases of hotel rooms, turning their familiar banality into something strange by the tidy little marks of his technique.

René Magritte
Forbidden Reproduction, 1937

The Surrealists subverted the traditional calm
and comfort of the interior to create images
that shock and surprise. In this portrait of the
art collector Edward James Magritte plays
with the conventional view in the mirror.

Dorothea Tanning
Eine Kleine Nachtmusik, 1943

A corridor, doors, a stairway, all
conventional ingredients of a home,
are the setting for the inexplicable
happenings of a nightmare.

what happened next? 177

Richard Hamilton
Just what is it that makes today's homes so different, so appealing?, 1956

Hamilton's iconic work assembles a collection of items of domesticity and popular culture, from TV to tape recorder, that seem so necessary to the homemakers of the consumer society.

The bourgeois domesticity associated with the interior was held up for disapproving inspection by the feminist artists of the 1970s. Whereas the Surrealists turned the interior's familiarity on its head with their disorientating images, the feminists questioned its conventional face. They found in the domestic interior an irresistible subject and had much to say about it, producing work that showed the home as the site of their oppression and not as a place of nurture. In the legendary but sadly destroyed Womanhouse in Los Angeles in 1972, Sandy Orgel created an installation of a woman confined within the shelves of a linen closet, a representation of imprisoned womanhood that recalls Degas' portrait of Hélène Rouart trapped behind her father's chair. In *Semiotics of the Kitchen*, a video work of 1975, the American artist Martha Rosler bangs, crashes, stabs and points her kitchen utensils, her ever more frantic and violent actions at war with the calm commentary that names them alphabetically. It is the same subject matter as the housewives of seventeenth-century Dutch interiors or of Vallotton's *Woman Searching Through a Cupboard*, but looked at from a critical feminist point of view. As time passed and feminist theories deepened and became more complex, a new generation of artists questioned the depiction of the home as solely a place of oppression and suggested some of its pleasures. In Rebecca Horn's wittily poetic installation, *El Rio de la Luna: Room of Lovers, Barcelona* (1992), the lovers are represented by the bed and the mechanical bows of the violins that make romantic music. Since 1980, the room has made frequent appearances in installation art. Louise Bourgeois, for example, has constructed rooms that explore ideas of memory, sexuality, lies and fears. *Cell (You Better Grow*

Sandy Orgel
Linen Closet, 1972

The now destroyed Womanhouse in Los Angeles was home to a legendary collection of installations by the first wave of feminist artists. Orgel's woman trapped in her linen closet is critical about the role of women in the home.

Martha Rosler
Semiotics of the Kitchen, 1975

The domestic interior is a potent subject
for twentieth-century artists. This video
work by an American feminist presents
the reverse view of the kitchen scenes
that began with the Dutch masters
of the seventeenth century. Instead
of equating good housekeeping
with admirable moral values, Rosler
bangs and crashes her utensils as
she names them, expressing anger
at the housewife's role.

Up), 1993, one of a series of cell rooms made in the years
around 1990, includes a disturbing pairing of white plaster
arms and a 1930s dressing-table mirror.

It is not only members of the major art movements who
have shown interest in the domestic interior, but also loner
artists. Perhaps one of the most eloquent was the American
Edward Hopper, whose rooms are the true heroes of his
images, for they explain his subjects both emotionally as well
as realistically. The almost featureless settings suggest the
mental isolation of his figures. The single pieces of furniture
and the static views from the windows suggest their empty
lives. And the blocks of sunlight on the walls and floors
suggest the heaviness of time that refuses to pass. Like
Hammershøi, Hopper was an artist who found rooms
and their associations exciting. Occasionally, he painted
rooms with no one in them at all and occasionally, as in
Night Windows (1928), with its pink-clad woman viewed
from behind, he revealed his understanding of their
voyeuristic element.

Today, the interior is everywhere, from the paintings
of women in bright and sunny rooms, as technically
competent, visually pleasurable and intellectually
undemanding as watching Fred and Ginger dance,
to the allusive, almost abstract paintings of rooms by
Matthias Weischer shown at the 2005 Venice Biennale.
As the newspapers say, reports of its death are premature.

Rebecca Horn

El Rio de la Luna: Room of Lovers, Barcelona,
1992

Created for the Hotel Peninsular in
Barcelona, Horn's installation is both
witty and romantic in its allusions to the
music of love and to the female body as a
violin in terms of shape and its capacity
to be 'played' by the lover. The room
with its closed door and window evokes
the setting necessary for a scene of
private pleasures.

Opposite: **Edward Hopper**
Night Windows, 1928

The theme of one or two figures in a
room fascinated this American painter,
whether it was an office, hotel or,
as here, a domestic interior. In this
room, glimpsed from outside on a
warm summer night, a woman is
seen in a state of partial undress,
revealing Hopper's understanding of
the subject's voyeuristic possibilities.

Matthias Weischer
Erfundener Mann, 2003

Weischer's interest in ambiguous spaces
and his refined colour sense prove that
the interior's visual possibilities remain
unexhausted. The title refers to the
imaginary seated figure constructed
from such familiar domestic objects as
a painting and a shape that reminds
the viewer of a bowl.

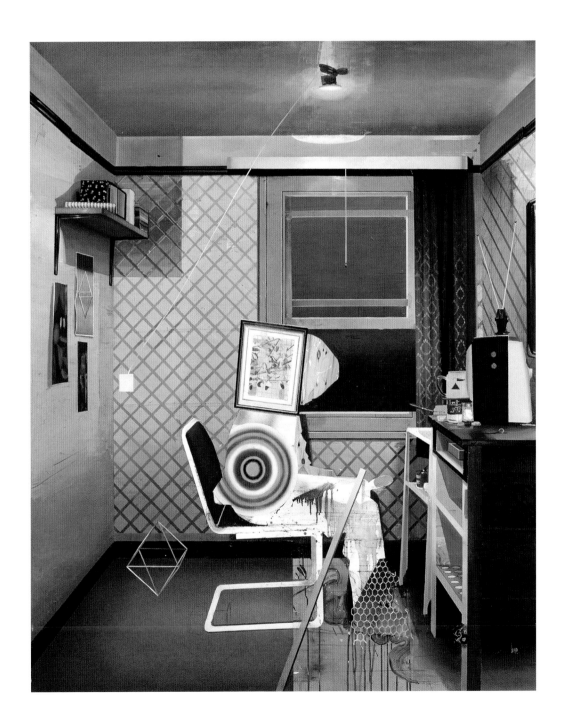

conclusion

Of course, the domestic interior did not, will not, cannot die. It is a subject too enmeshed with ourselves. It has been art's little secret, all the more powerful for not being admitted. Nobody in authority wants to claim it, neither the theoreticians of the seventeenth and eighteenth centuries nor the art historians of the twentieth. For the earlier ones, it was beneath their notice, incapable of carrying the important ideas they hoped would make painting as serious an art as poetry. For the later ones, it was an irrelevance because a subject was not what art was about, particularly not a subject that stood for everything avant-garde art was not – bourgeois, familiar, acceptable. Its emergence around 1900 was never properly registered by the growing audience who embraced looking at art as a popular spectator sport.

How did it manage to get so lost? I have no answer but I do have two suggestions. The first, which I have explored through this book, is that the interior was hidden away in genre painting, in the reclining nude and under portraiture. Aside from a brief acknowledgement at the end of the nineteenth century when French critics defined the newness of the art of Vuillard, Bonnard and Vallotton as *intimiste*, the interior has been made invisible by being hijacked by the genres that are fine art's way of classifying paintings.

My second suggestion is more personal. I think the reason it has taken so long for us to notice the interior is information overload. Scholarship is valuable, but sometimes it can blind us to the beauty of a work. It is thanks to scholarship that we know that certain features of *The Arnolfini Portrait* are intended to convey meaning.

Scholars can explain why only one candle is lit in the chandelier – it marks the presence of Christ in the room; why the figure of St Margaret, the saint who hears the prayers of childbirth, sits atop a bedpost – to suggest this is a marriage contract of some kind; why the dog is included – it is an age-old Christian symbol of fidelity. Art is a language and painters know how to use it.

But artists are not merely concerned with imparting a message. They have eyes as well as intellect. They give us the gift of their vision by showing us what we don't see or what we see but cannot reproduce. In the hands of painters particularly sensitive to the interior, this can evolve into something strange and beautiful, which helps the viewer see things previously ignored or taken for granted. This means that despite the explanations of *The Arnolfini Portrait* as a record of a formal union, it also exists on a level of the simplest visual pleasure, that of recognition of an artist's skill in reproducing reality in a way that makes us see afresh. The light that fills this peaceful room and sculpts the roundness of the oranges arrests a moment of the 1430s. 'Jan van Eyck was here' wrote the artist in Latin on the surface of his painting, right in the centre below the circular mirror. We know that it refers to his act of witnessing a contract but we tend to forget that it also refers to his act of transferring his observations into paint, a painstaking procedure which in itself adds to the solemnity of the scene. Interesting though it is, all the scholarship in the world does not increase the miracle Van Eyck achieved in making this interior a hymn to the delights of sight as much as a part of the programme of the painting.

Jan van Eyck
The Arnolfini Portrait, 1434

This is where it all began. Van Eyck's sensitivity to the effect of light coming through the window reveals an artist who understands the special qualities of the interior. He is the forebear of all the artists in this book.

We have been so intimidated by scholars that we have to learn to trust ourselves again. Are those cloths by Mary's chair in the *Virgin and Child* from Campin's workshop the ancestors of the nappies we use today? Such questions may not be scholarly but they are human. We search interiors like these for information about our predecessors, and the pleasure this affords should not be dented by our sophisticated art-historical selves who have been taught to think that artists include only what furthers their story, clarifies its message and follows tradition.

Art historians have told us that it was through the images of seventeenth-century Holland that the first middle-class society pictured its values and aspirations. Scholars may explain the hidden morality behind the interiors of these works, but what we love – and have to learn to admit we love – is the peace and tidiness of those rooms, their brass-studded chairs, the air around the furniture, above the heads, below the ceiling, and the artists' magic power to transmit sound down through the centuries: leather soles on tiled floors receding through open doors, the clink of glasses and the strains of music. If we had the courage to admit that it is our eyes and not our brains that are affected by these works and that we take pleasure in the surfaces of slippery satin dresses and gleaming drinking glasses held up to catch the light, perhaps the interior would not have been lost to us.

Research has made sophisticates of us all by teaching us to question the reality of what we see in paintings. But though we know that much of what we observe comes out of the artist's head, or is copied from studio props or rearranged in the interest of composition, colour or message, we would be stupid to forget that it must contain a general truth to satisfy the clients of the time. Research into seventeenth-century Dutch inventories has shown that, contrary to the information in the paintings, carpets, tapestries and musical instruments were in short supply among the wealthy and their homes were more cluttered than they appear in art.[1] But even if not one painted Dutch interior ever matched a real one, if they had not looked convincing at some level, they would probably never have been bought.

We must remember that paintings have powers that have nothing to do with art history. Rothenstein's *The Browning Readers* of 1900 was admired as a guide to taste: 'Many people, to my knowledge [wrote a lady to the press] were deeply impressed by this simple and beautiful arrangement, and resolved to have no more serried ranks of framed photographs, clocks, bronzes of poor design, and undistinguished china. For this reform, I think some of the credit should go to Mr William Rothenstein for showing us how infinitely more attractive a simple arrangement could be.'[2]

But it is not just realistic rooms that we must learn to see afresh. The same refusal to see what is before our eyes has occurred with the art of the last hundred years. Instead of being dazzled by the scholarship that decodes the meaning of the early works, we are now dazzled by the knowledgeable who explain the 'isms' of modern art. We can see that Matisse paints rooms, but in our respectful appreciation of his flatness, line and colour we overlook the transformative eye and hand that can turn the surroundings of our lives into something we recognize but made stranger and more beautiful. It almost feels like heresy to suggest that maybe part of the pleasure of enjoying Matisse – or Bonnard, Louise Bourgeois, Rachel Whiteread or any of the dozens of modern and contemporary artists who work with the interior – is that we understand their starting point. When we ignore the subject that inspires the artists, we deny ourselves the chance to broaden our perception of life as well as art and we deny them their place in the long line of artists of the interior.

Rooms are the shells of our lives. They are built to our scale and we understand them whatever era they are from. The truth is that the domestic interior is as close to us as our clothes. Luckily for us, there have always been artists with the understanding and the power to transmit this into art.

notes

Introduction: 1900

1 'Interiors and Still-lifes' in *1900: Art at the Crossroads*, exh. cat., London, Royal Academy of Arts, New York, Harry N. Abrams, 2000, p.224; Kenneth McConkey, 'New English Intimisme: The Painting of the Edwardian Interior' in *The Edwardians: Secrets and Desires*, exh. cat., Canberra, National Gallery of Australia, 2004.

2   Looking for the Interior

1 For a discussion of Hoogstraten's ideas see Celeste Brusati, *Artifice and Illusion: The Art and Writing of Samuel van Hoogstraten*, University of Chicago Press, 1995.

2 *The Artists Assistant*, 3rd edn, London, R. Sayor, 1772, pp.11 and 12.

3 Henry Murray, *The Art of Portrait Painting in Oil Colours*, 2nd edn, London, Winsor and Newton, 1851, p.54.

4 Ibid., p.56.

5 Ibid., p.61.

6 Sir Joshua Reynolds, *Discourses on Art*, ed. Robert R. Wark, New Haven and London, Yale University Press, 1975, Discourse 3, 1770, p.44.

7 Kenneth Clark, *Landscape into Art*, London, John Murray, 1949, p.26.

8 John Ingamells and John Edgcumbe (eds), *The Letters of Sir Joshua Reynolds*, New Haven and London, Yale University Press, 2000, pp.100–1.

9 Sir Joshua Reynolds, *Discourses on Art*, op. cit., Discourse 4, 1771, p.69.

10 Ibid., pp.70–1.

11 Ibid., p.62.

12 Henry Fuseli, *Lectures on Painting*, London, Cadell and Davies, 1820, fourth lecture, 'Invention', p.194.

13 Ibid., pp.185–6.

14 Thomas Phillips, *Lectures on the History and Principles of Painting*, London, Longman, 1833, lecture 7, 'On Composition', p.329.

15 Jakob Rosenberg, Seymour Slive and E.H. ter Kuile (eds), *Dutch Art and Architecture 1600–1800*, The Pelican History of Art, Harmondsworth, Penguin, 1966, pp.18–19.

16 Ibid., p.19.

17 Carol Duncan, 'Happy Mothers and Other New Ideas in Eighteenth-Century French Art', in Norma Broude and Mary D. Garrard (eds), *Feminism and Art History*, New York and London, Harper & Row, 1982.

18 Colin B. Bailey (ed.), *The Age of Watteau, Chardin and Fragonard: Masterpieces of French Genre Painting*, exh. cat., New Haven and London, Yale University Press in association with the National Gallery of Canada, Ottowa, 2003, p.4.

19 Lorenz Eitner, *Neoclassicism and Romanticism, 1750–1850*, vol.1, Sources and Documents in the History of Art series, Englewood Cliffs, NJ, Prentice-Hall, 1970, p.53.

3   The Secret Life of the Interior

1 *Polite Society by Arthur Devis, 1712–1787. Portraits of the English Country Gentleman and his Family*, exh. cat., Preston, Harris Museum and Art Gallery, 1983, p.46.

4   The Unpeopled Interior

1 Charlotte Gere, *Nineteenth Century Interiors*, London, Thames & Hudson, 1992.

2 Philippe Aries, *Centuries of Childhood* (1960), trans. Robert Baldick, Harmondsworth, Penguin, 1973, p.385.

3 John Tosh, *A Man's Place: Masculinity and the Middle-Class Home in Victorian England*, New Haven and London, Yale University Press, 1999, p.4.

4 *The Complete Letters of Vincent van Gogh*, vol.3, 2nd edn, London, Thames & Hudson, 1999, p.86.

5 Mary Taubman, *Gwen John*, London, Scolar Press, 1985, p.112.

5   Seeing the Light

1 Martha Kapos (ed.), *The Impressionists: A Retrospective*, New York and London, Hugh Lauter Levin Associates, 1991, p.101.

2 Claude Keisch and Marie Ursula Riemann-Reyher (eds), *Adolph Menzel 1815–1905: Between Romanticism and Impressionism*, exh. cat., New Haven and London, Yale University Press in association with the National Gallery of Art, Washington, 1996, p.214.

6   The Portrait Interior

1 Nicholas Penny (ed.), *Reynolds*, exh. cat., London, Royal Academy of Arts in association with Weidenfeld and Nicolson, 1986, p.57.

2 Sir Joshua Reynolds, *Discourses on Art*, ed. Robert R. Wark, New Haven and London, Yale University Press, 1975, Discourse 7, 1776, p.140.

3 *Magazine of Art*, vol. 2, new series, 1903–4, p.212.

4 Everett Raymond Kinstler, Susan E. Meyer (ed.), *Painting Portraits*, New York, Watson-Guptill, 1971, p.97.

5 Christian Witt-Dörring, 'Domestic Life' in *Vienna in the Age of Schubert: The Biedermeier Interior 1815–1848*, exh. cat., London, Elron Press in association with the Victoria and Albert Museum, 1979, p.27.

6 Rosalind P. Gray, *Russian Genre Painting in the Nineteenth Century*, Oxford and New York, Oxford University Press, 2000, p.125.

7 Mario Praz, *An Illustrated History of Interior Decoration*, trans. William Weaver, London, Thames & Hudson, 1964, p.277.

8 Andrea Rose, *Pre-Raphaelite Portraits*, Yeovil, Oxford Illustrated Press, 1981, p.66.

9 Charles Saumarez Smith, *The National Portrait Gallery*, London, National Portrait Gallery, 1997, p.150.

10 Lorenz Eitner, *Neoclassicism and Romanticism, 1750–1850*, vol.2, Sources and Documents in the History of Art series, Englewood Cliffs, NJ, Prentice-Hall, 1970, p.155.

11 Linda Nochlin, *Realism and Tradition in Art, 1848–1900*, Sources and Documents in the History of Art series, Englewood Cliffs, NJ, Prentice-Hall, 1966, pp.83–4.

12 Elizabeth Gilmore Holt (ed.), *The Expanding World of Art, 1874–1902*, vol.1, part 2, New Haven and London, Yale University Press, 1988, p.199.

13 Robert L. Herbert, *Impressionism: Art, Leisure and Parisian Society*, New Haven and London, Yale University Press, 1988, p.29.

14 William Rothenstein, *Men and Memories: Recollections of William Rothenstein*, vol.1, *1872–1900*, London, Faber & Faber, 1931, pp.162–3.

15 Richard Ormond and Elaine Kilmurray, *John Singer Sargent: Complete Paintings*, vol.2, *Portraits of the 1890s*, New Haven and London, Yale University Press, 2002, p.155.

16 Norman and Jeanne MacKenzie (eds), *The Diary of Beatrice Webb*, vol. 4, *1924–1943*, *The Wheel of Life*, London, Virago in association with the London School of Economics and Political Science; Cambridge, MA, Harvard University Press, 1985, p.143.

17 Kenneth McConkey, *Sir John Lavery*, Edinburgh, Cannongate, 1993, p.169.

18 Ibid.

19 Herbert Furst, *Portrait Painting, Its Nature and Function*, London, John Lane, 1927, p.127.

7   The Moral Interior

1 Thomas Gisborne, *An Enquiry into the Duties of the Female Sex*, 11th edn, London, Cadell and Davies, 1816, pp.315–6, 343, 347.

2 Sharon Marcus, *Apartment Stories: City and Home in Nineteenth-Century Paris and London*, Berkeley, University of California Press, 1999, p.151.

3 J.W. Kirton, *Happy Homes and How to Make Them*, Birmingham, 1870, p.155.

4 Ibid., p.121.

5 Robert Kerr, *The Gentleman's House or How to Plan English Residences from the Parsonage to the Palace*, London, John Murray, 1864, p.81.

6 Ibid., p.119.

7 Ibid.

8 Ibid., p.143.

9 John Ruskin, *The Times*, 5 May 1854, reproduced in Linda Nochlin, *Realism and Tradition in Art, 1848–1900*, op. cit., pp.126–7.

10 Rosalind P. Gray, *Russian Genre Painting in the Nineteenth Century*, op. cit., p.137.

11 Linda Nochlin, *Realism and Tradition in Art*, op. cit., pp.150–1.

12 Anna Gruetzner Robins and Richard Thomson, *Degas, Sickert and Toulouse-Lautrec: London and Paris 1870–1910*, exh. cat., London, Tate, 2005, p.196.

13 Pamela M. Fletcher, *Narrating Modernity: The British Problem Picture 1895–1914*, Aldershot, Ashgate, 2003, p.1.

14 Ibid., p.64.

15 L.V. Fildes, *Luke Fildes, A Victorian Painter*, London, Michael Joseph, 1968, p.118.

16 Alice Meynell, 'Newlyn', *Art Journal*, new series, London, 1889, p.100.

8   The Artist's Own Interior

1 Martha Kapos (ed.), *The Impressionists: A Retrospective*, op. cit., p.100.

2 Robert Kerr, *The Gentleman's House*, op. cit., p.119.

3 Richard Kendall (ed.), *Monet by Himself*, London, Macdonald Orbis, 1989, p.26.

4 Gloria Groom, 'Interiors and Portraits' in *Gustave Caillebotte: Urban Impressionist*, New York, Abbeville, 1995, p.178. Published to accompany an exhibition at the Galeries Nationales du Grand Palais, Paris, The Art Institute of Chicago and Los Angeles County Museum of Art.

5   David Cecil, *Jane Austen*, Cambridge University Press, 1935, pp.13–14.
6   Elizabeth Gilmore Holt, *The Expanding World of Art*, op. cit., p.210.
7   *The Letters and Journals of Paula Modersohn-Becker*, trans. and annotated by J. Diane Radycki, Metuchen, NJ, and London, Scarecrow Press, 1980, p.113.
8   Ibid., p.115.

9   Coming of Age
1   Edward J. Poynter, *Ten Lectures on Art*, London, Chapman and Hall, 1879, p.86.
2   Edward Armitage, *Lectures on Painting*, lecture 12, 'Composition of Incident Pictures', London, Trübner, 1883, p.238.
3   Poul Vad, *Vilhelm Hammershøi and Danish Art at the Turn of the Century*, trans. Kenneth Tindall, New Haven and London, Yale University Press, 1992, p.401.
4   Ibid.
5   Laurene Buckley, *Edmund C. Tarbell: Poet of Domesticity*, New York, Hudson Hills Press, 2001, p.97.

6   William Rothenstein, *Men and Memories*, op. cit., p.349.
7   William Rothenstein, *Men and Memories: Recollections of William Rothenstein*, vol.2, *1900–1922*, London, Faber & Faber, 1932, p.2.
8   William Rothenstein, *Men and Memories*, vol.1, op. cit., p. 347.
9   *Art Journal*, 1908, p.20.
10   *The Studio*, February–September 1909, vol.46–47, p.183.
11   *Art Journal*, 1908, p.31.
12   *The Studio*, September 1909, vol.46–47, pp.251–9.
13   For example, G. Stork, *Gazette des Beaux-Arts*, vol.135, no.1575 (April 2000), pp.255–64; N. Forgione, 'The Shadow Only: Shadow and Silhouette in Late Nineteenth Century Paris', *Art Bulletin*, vol.81, no.3 (September 1999), pp.490–512.
14   Walter Richard Sickert, *New Age*, 2 June 1910.
15   *Magazine of Art*, vol.24, 1900–1, p.364.
16   Belinda Thomson, 'Bonnard and Vuillard: For and Against Their Pairing' in Jörg Zutter (ed.), *Pierre Bonnard: Observing Nature*, exh. cat., Canberra, National Gallery of Australia, 2003, p.153.
17   *Bonnard and His Environment*, exh. cat., New York, Museum of Modern Art, 1964, p.22.

10   What Happened Next?
1   Christopher Reed (ed.), *Not at Home, The Suppression of Domesticity in Modern Art and Architecture*, London, Thames & Hudson, 1996, p.15.
2   Bruce Arnold, *Orpen: Mirror to an Age*, London, Jonathan Cape, 1981, p.239.
3   Guy Cogeval et al., *Edouard Vuillard*, exh. cat., New Haven and London, Yale University Press in association with Montreal Museum of Fine Arts and the National Gallery of Art, Washington, 2003, p.356.
4   David Sylvester (ed.), *René Magritte*, catalogue raisonné, vol.3, London, Philip Wilson, 1993, p.378.

Conclusion
1   Klaske Muizelaar and Derek Phillips, *Picturing Men and Women in the Dutch Golden Age: Paintings and People in Historical Perspective*, New Haven and London, Yale University Press, 2003, p.54.
2   Robert Speaight, *William Rothenstein: The Portrait of an Artist in His Time*, London, Eyre & Spottiswoode, 1962, p.149.

select bibliography

Since so little has been written about the domestic interior in paintings, much of my information was found in books about realism or genre painting, in the occasional exhibition catalogue and in monographs about relevant artists. Books that had a direct bearing on the text are cited in the notes. Many of the most helpful books I read were tangential to the subject, for example, histories of interior decoration and social histories of the home, and I have listed a selection of these here.

Painting
The Absent Presence: The Uninhabited Interior in Nineteenth and Twentieth Century British Art, exh. cat., Sheffield City Art Galleries, 1991

The Artistic Interior – Studios and Rooms in English and European Art c.1850–1920, exh. cat., London, Christopher Wood Gallery, 1991

Barnes, J., 'Bonnard's Interiors', *Modern Painters*, 11:2 (Summer 1998)

Baron, Wendy, *The Camden Town Group*, London, Scolar Press, 1979

Beckett, Jane, 'The Abstract Interior' in *Towards a New Art: Essays on the Background to Abstract Art, 1910–20*, London, Tate Gallery, 1980, pp.90–124

Bonnard and His Environment, exh. cat., New York, Museum of Modern Art, 1964

Chu, Petra ten-Doesschate, *French Realism and the Dutch Masters*, Utrecht, Haentjens Dekker & Gumbert, 1974

Dewing, David (ed.), *Home and Garden, Paintings and Drawings of English, Middle-Class, Urban Domestic Spaces, 1675–1914*, exh. cat., London, Geffrye Museum, 2003

Easton, Elizabeth W., *The Intimate Interiors of Edouard Vuillard*, London, Thames & Hudson, 1989

Gere, Charlotte, *Nineteenth Century Interiors*, London, Thames & Hudson, 1992

Groom, Gloria, *Beyond the Easel, Decorative Painting by Bonnard, Vuillard, Denis and Roussel, 1890–1930*, exh. cat., New Haven and London, Yale University Press, 2001

Herbert, Robert L., *Impressionism: Art, Leisure and Parisian Society*, New Haven and London, Yale University Press, 1988

Interiors from the Collection of the Art Gallery of New South Wales, exh. cat., Sydney, AGNSW, 1981

Les Peintres du Silence, exh. cat., Hotel de Ville de Bruxelles, 2001

Richard Hamilton: Interiors 1964–1979, exh. cat., London, Waddington Galleries, 1979

Rand, Richard, *Intimate Encounters: Love and Domesticity in Eighteenth-Century France*, exh. cat., Hanover, NH, Hood Museum of Art, Dartmouth College and Princeton, NJ, Princeton University Press

Reed, Christopher (ed.), *Not at Home, The Suppression of Domesticity in Modern Art and Architecture*, London, Thames & Hudson, 1996

—, *Bloomsbury Rooms: Modernism, Subculture and Domesticity*, New Haven and London, Yale University Press, 2004

Rodwell, Jenny, *Painting Interiors*, London, Collins, 1989

Sidlauskas, Susan, *Body, Self and Place in Nineteenth-Century Painting*, Cambridge University Press, 2000

Todd, Pamela, *The Impressionists at Home*, London, Thames & Hudson, 2005

Varnedoe, Kirk, *Northern Light: Nordic Art at the Turn of the Century*, New Haven and London, Yale University Press, 1988

Walter Gay: A Retrospective, New York, Grey Art Gallery and Study Center, NYU, 1980

Weinberg, H. Barbara, et al., *American Realism and Impressionism: The Painting of Modern Life 1885–1915*, exh. cat., New York, Metropolitan Museum of Art, 1994

Zaczek, Iain, *Impressionist Interiors*, London, Studio Editions, 1993

Decoration
Cornforth, John, *English Interiors 1790–1848*, London, Barrie & Jenkins, 1978

Dutton, Ralph, *The English Interior 1500–1900*, London, Batsford, 1948

Forge, Suzanne, *Victorian Splendour: Australian Interior Decoration 1837–1901*, Oxford University Press, 1981

Praz, Mario, *An Illustrated History of Interior Decoration*, London, Thames & Hudson, 1964

Smith, Charles Saumarez, *Eighteenth-Century Decoration: Design and the Domestic Interior in England*, London, Weidenfeld and Nicolson, 1993

Social History
Bachelard, Gaston, *The Poetics of Space*, trans. Maria Jolas, New York, Orion Press, 1964

Best, Sue, 'Sexualizing Space' in Elizabeth Grosz and Elspeth Probyn (eds), *Sexy Bodies: The Strange Carnalities of Feminism*, London, Routledge, 1995

Clark, Clifford E., *The American Family Home: 1800–1960*, Chapel Hill, University of North Carolina Press, 1986

Davidoff, Leonore, *The Best Circles: Society, Etiquette and the Season*, London, Croom Helm, 1973

Davidoff, Leonore and Catherine Hall (eds), *Family Fortunes: Men and Women of the English Middle Class 1750–1850*, Chicago, University of Chicago Press; London, Hutchinson, 1987

Donald, Moira, 'Tranquil Havens?' in Inga Bryden and Janet Floyd (eds), *Domestic Space: Reading the Nineteenth-Century Interior*, Manchester University Press, 1999

Marcus, Sharon, *Apartment Stories: City and Home in Nineteenth-Century Paris and London*, Berkeley, University of California Press, 1999

list of illustrations

Dimensions of works are given in centimetres then inches, height before width.

p.72 Georg Friedrich Kersting, *Man Reading by Lamplight*, 1814. Oil on canvas, 47.5 x 37 (18¾ x 14⅝). Oskar Reinhart Foundation, Winterthur
p.73 Wilhelm Bendz, *A Smoking Party*, 1827–8. Oil on canvas, 98.5 x 85 (38¾ x 33½). Photo akg-images
p.74 Adolph Menzel, *Living Room with the Artist's Sister*, 1847. Oil on paper, board backing, 46.1 x 51.7 (18⅛ x 20⅜). Bayerische Staatsgemaldesammlungen, Neue Pinakothek, Munich
p.75 Robert Braithwaite Martineau, *The Last Chapter*, 1863. Oil on canvas, 71.5 x 41.9 (28½ x 16½). Birmingham Museums & Art Gallery
p.76 Félix Vallotton, *Nude at the Stove*, 1900. Gouache on board, 80 x 110 (31½ x 43¼). Private Collection
p.77 Carl Holsøe, *The Artist's Home at Lyngby*. Oil on canvas, 68.6 x 65.1 (27 x 25⅝). Christie's Images Ltd
p.79 English School, *Group Portrait of Three Men in an Interior, One Pointing to South America on a Globe*, early 19th century. Oil on canvas, 114.8 x 107.3 (45¼ x 42¼). Christie's Images Ltd
p.80 Wilhelm Bendz, *Interior in the Amaliegade*, 1830. Oil on canvas, 32.3 x 49 (12¾ x 19¼). Den Hirschsprungske Samling, Copenhagen
p.82 Friedrich von Amerling, *Rudolf von Arthaber with his Children Rudolf, Emilie and Gustav Looking at the Portrait of their Deceased Mother*, 1837. Oil on canvas, 221 x 555 (87 x 61). Österreichische Galerie, Vienna. Courtesy of Bridgeman Art Library
p.83 Emilius Ditlev Baerentzen, *Winther Family*, 1827. Oil on canvas, 70.5 x 65.5 (27¾ x 25¾). National Gallery of Scotland, Edinburgh. Courtesy of Bridgeman Art Library
p.84 Aleksei Venetsianov, *Prince V.P. Kochubei in his Study*, *c.*1834. Oil on canvas, 144 x 106 (56¾ x 41¾). State Russian Museum, St Petersburg
p.85 Fyodor Petrovich Tolstoy, *Portrait of a Family*, 1830. Oil on canvas, 89 x 117 (35 x 46⅛). State Hermitage Museum, St Petersburg
p.86 Kapiton Zelentsov, *Interior*, late 1820s. Oil on canvas, 37 x 45.5 (14⅝ x 17⅞). State Tretyakov Gallery, Moscow
p.87 Prokofy Yegorovich Pushkarev, *At Home*. State Tretyakov Gallery, Moscow
p.88 John Everett Millais, *James Wyatt and his Granddaughter Mary Wyatt*, 1849. Oil on panel, 35.2 x 45 (13⅞ x 17¾). Collection Andrew Lloyd Webber
p.89 Henry Treffry Dunn, *Dante Gabriel Rossetti and Theodore Watts-Dunton*, 1882. Gouache, 54 x 81.9 (21¼ x 32¼). Courtesy of the National Portrait Gallery, London
pp.90–1 Robert S. Tait, *A Chelsea Interior*, 1858. Oil on canvas, 86 x 57 (33⅞ x 22½). National Trust Photographic Library/Rob Matheson
p.92 Edouard Manet, *Emile Zola*, 1867. Oil on canvas, 146 x 114 (57½ x 44⅞). Musée d'Orsay, Paris
p.95 Edgar Degas, *Hélène Rouart in her Father's Study*, *c.*1886. Oil on canvas, 161 x 120 (63⅜ x 47¼). National Gallery, London
p.96 James Tissot, *Portrait of Mlle L.L.*, 1864. Oil on canvas, 124 x 99 (48⅞ x 39). Musée d'Orsay, Paris
p.97 James Tissot, *Frederick Gustavus Burnaby*, 1870. Oil on panel, 49.5 x 56.6 (19½ x 22⅓). Courtesy of the National Portrait Gallery, London
p.98 John Atkinson Grimshaw, *Dulce Domum*, 1885. Oil on canvas, 83.1 x 122.5 (32¾ x 48¼). Christie's Images Ltd, Courtesy Andrew Lloyd Webber Art Foundation
p.99 John Singer Sargent, *An Interior in Venice*, 1899. Oil on canvas, 64.8 x 80.6 (25½ x 31¾). Royal Academy of Arts, London
p.100 William Nicholson, *Sidney and Beatrice Webb*, 1928–9. Oil on canvas, 121.9 x 152 (48 x 59⅞). London School of Economics. Reproduced by permission of Elizabeth Banks
p.101 John Lavery, *A Quiet Day in the Studio*, 1883. Oil on canvas, 41.9 x 52.1 (16½ x 20½). Glasgow Museums, Kelvingrove Art Gallery and Museum. By Courtesy of Felix Rosenstiel's Widow & Son Ltd, London
p.102 John Lavery, *The Royal Family at Buckingham Palace*, 1913. Oil on canvas, 340 x 271 (134 x 107). Courtesy of the National Portrait Gallery, London. © Mr H.I. Spottiswoode (NPG 1745). By Courtesy of Felix Rosenstiel's Widow & Son Ltd, London
p.102 John Lavery, *The Studio Window, 7 July 1917*, 1917. Oil on canvas, 141.6 x 90.2 (55¾ x 35½). The Ulster Museum, Belfast. By Courtesy of Felix Rosenstiel's Widow & Son Ltd, London
p.103 John Lavery, *The Van Dyck Room, Wilton*, 1921. Oil on canvas, 25 x 30 (9⅞ x 11¾). Royal Academy of Arts, London. By Courtesy of Felix Rosenstiel's Widow & Son Ltd, London
p.105 Diego Velasquez, *Kitchen Scene with Christ in the House of Martha and Mary*, *c.*1618. Oil on canvas, 60 x 103.5 (23⅝ x 40¾). National Gallery, London
p.108 William Holman Hunt, *The Awakening Conscience*, 1853. Oil on canvas, 76.2 x 55.9 (30 x 22). Tate, London
p.109 Robert Braithwaite Martineau, *The Last Day in the Old Home*, 1862. Oil on canvas, 107.3 x 144.8 (42¼ x 57). Tate, London
p.110 Augustus Egg, *Past and Present No. 1*, 1858. Oil on canvas, 63.5 x 76.2 (25 x 30). Tate, London
p.111 George Elgar Hicks, *Woman's Mission: Companion of Manhood*, 1863. Oil on canvas, 76.2 x 64.1 (30 x 25¼). Tate, London 2005
p.112 James Tissot, *The Conservatory (The Rivals)*, *c.*1875–8. Oil on canvas, 42.5 x 53.9 (16¾ x 21¼). Private Collection
p.113 Pavel Fedotov, *The Major's Proposal*, 1848. Oil on canvas, 59 x 76 (23¼ x 29⅞). Photo akg-images
p.114 Adriano Cecioni, *Interior with a Figure*, *c.*1867. Oil on canvas, 28.5 x 35.5 (11¼ x 14). National Gallery of Modern Art, Rome
p.115 Odoardo Borrani, *Red Shirt Seamstresses*, 1863. Oil on canvas, 66 x 54 (26 x 21¼). Private Collection
p.116 Edgar Degas, *Interior*, 1868–9. Oil on canvas, 81 x 116 (31⅞ x 45⅝). Philadelphia Museum of Art. The Henry P. McIlhenny Collection. In memory of Frances P. McIlhenny
p.117 William Quiller Orchardson, *Mariage de Convenance*, 1883. Oil on canvas, 104.8 x 154.3 (41¼ x 60¾). Glasgow Museums, Kelvingrove Art Gallery and Museum
p.118 Luke Fildes, *The Doctor*, 1891. Oil on canvas, 166.4 x 241.9 (65½ x 95¼). Tate, London
p.119 Stanhope Forbes, *The Health of the Bride*, 1889. Oil on canvas, 152.5 x 200 (60 x 78¾). Tate, London © Courtesy of the artist's estate/Bridgeman Art Library
pp.120–21 Frank Bramley, *The Hopeless Dawn*, 1888. Oil on canvas, 122.6 x 167.6 (48 x 66). Tate, London
p.122 Lawrence Alma-Tadema, *A Silent Greeting*, 1889. Oil on panel, 30.5 x 23 (12 x 9). Tate, London
p.123 Rowland Holyoake, *The Connoisseur*, *c.*1893. 76 x 54.5 (30 x 21½). Christie's Images Ltd
p.125 Gustaf Cederström, *An Interior with a Woman Reading by a Table*, 1897. Oil on canvas, 55 x 46.4 (21¾ x 18½). Christie's Images Ltd
p.126 Mary Cassatt, *Tea*, 1879–80. Oil on canvas, 64.7 x 92.7 (25½ x 36½). Museum of Fine Arts, Boston
p.127 Edgar Degas, *The Pedicure*, 1873. Essence on paper mounted on canvas, 61 x 46 (24 x 18⅛). Musée d'Orsay, Paris
p.129 Claude Monet, *The Luncheon*, 1868. Oil on canvas, 230 x 150 (90 x 59). Städelsches Kunstinstitut, Frankfurt
p.130 Claude Monet, *Meditation: Mme Monet on a Sofa*, 1871. Oil on canvas, 48 x 75 (18⅞ x 29½). Musée d'Orsay, Paris
p.131 Claude Monet, *Apartment Interior*, 1875. Oil on canvas, 81.5 x 60.5 (32⅛ x 23⅞). Musée d'Orsay, Paris
p.132 Gustave Caillebotte, *Luncheon*, 1876. Oil on canvas, 52 x 75 (20½ x 29½). Private Collection
p.133 Gustave Caillebotte, *Young Man Playing the Piano*, 1876. Oil on canvas, 80 x 116 (31½ x 45⅝). Private Collection
p.134 Edouard Manet, *Reading*, 1868. Oil on canvas, 60.5 x 73.5 (23⅞ x 29). Musée d'Orsay, Paris
p.135 Gustave Caillebotte, *Portrait of a Man*, 1877. Oil on canvas, 81 x 100 (31⅞ x 39⅜). Christie's Images Ltd
p.136 Edouard Vuillard, *The Painter Ker-Xavier Roussel and his Daughter*, 1903. Oil on canvas, 58.2 x 53 (22⅞ x 20⅞). Collection Albright-Knox Art Gallery, Buffalo. Room of Contemporary Art Fund, 1934. © ADAGP, Paris and DACS, London 2006
p.138 James Ensor, *Ostende Afternoon*, 1881. Oil on canvas, 108 x 133 (42½ x 52⅜). Koninklijk Museum voor Schone Kunsten, Antwerp. © DACS 2006
p.139 James Ensor, *The Oyster Eater*, 1882. Oil on canvas, 207 x 150 (81½ x 59). Koninklijk Museum voor Schone Kunsten, Antwerp. © DACS 2006
p.140 Kitty Kielland, *Studio Interior*, Paris, 1883. Oil on canvas, 42.5 x 36.8 (16¼ x 14½). Kunstmuseum, Lillehammer
p.141 P.S. Krøyer, *Interior, Marie Krøyer Painting*, 1890. Oil on canvas, 15 x 18.7 (5⅞ x 7⅜). Skagens Museum, Denmark
p.141 Spencer Gore, *Interior, 31 Mornington Crescent*, 1910. Oil on canvas, 50.8 x 60.9 (20 x 24). Leeds Museums and Galleries, City Art Gallery/Bridgeman Art Library
pp.142–3 Ilya Repin, *Study of a Family Portrait*, 1905. Oil on canvas, 87.6 x 179.7 (34½ x 70¾). Christie's Images Ltd
p.145 Mariya Yakunchikova-Weber, *Covers* (detail)
p.146 Harriet Backer, *The Library of Thorvold Boeck*, 1902. Oil on canvas, 94.5 x 89 (37¼ x 35). National Gallery, Oslo
p.147 Adolf Heinrich-Hansen, *A Woman Reading in an Interior*, 1918. 52.3 x 44.5 (20⅝ x 17½). Christie's Images Ltd

p.148 Pierre Bonnard, *The Meal*, 1899. Oil on board, 32 x 40 (12⅝ x 15¾). Private Collection. © ADAGP, Paris and DACS, London 2006

p.148 Pierre Bonnard, *Man and Woman*, 1900. Oil on canvas, 115 x 72 (45¼ x 28⅜). Musée d'Orsay, Paris. © ADAGP, Paris and DACS, London 2006

p.149 Pierre Bonnard, *The Bathroom Mirror*, 1908. Oil on panel, 120 x 97 (47¼ x 38¼). Pushkin State Museum of Fine Arts, Moscow. © ADAGP, Paris and DACS, London 2006

p.150 Félix Vallotton, *Woman Doing her hair*, 1900. Tempera on board, 61 x 81 (24 x 31⅞). Musée des Beaux-Arts, Dijon, inv. 4751

p.151 Félix Vallotton, *The Top Hat*, 1887. Oil on canvas, 32.5 x 24.5 (12¾ x 9⅝). Private Collection

p.151 Félix Vallotton, *Woman Searching Through a Cupboard*, 1900. Oil on canvas, 78 x 49.5 (30¾ x 19½). Private Collection, Basel

p.152 Henri Matisse, *Woman Reading*, 1895. Oil on wooden panel, 61.5 x 48 (24¼ x 18⅞). Musée National d'Art Moderne, Centre Georges Pompidou, Paris. © Succession H. Matisse/DACS 2006

p.152 Henri Matisse, *Girl Reading*, 1905–6. Oil on canvas, 72.7 x 59.4 (28⅝ x 23⅜). Private Collection, New York. © Succession H. Matisse/DACS 2006

p.153 Anna Ancher, *Sunshine in the Blue Room*, 1891. Oil on canvas, 65.2 x 58.8 (25⅝ x 23¼). Photo akg-images

p.154 Carl Holsøe, *In the Dining Room*. 85 x 67.3 (33½ x 26½). Christie's Images Ltd

p.155 Carl Holsøe, *An Interior with a Cello*. Oil on canvas, 75.5 x 61.8 (29¾ x 24¼). Christie's Images Ltd

p.156 Harriet Backer, *By Lamplight*, 1890. Oil on canvas, 64.7 x 66.5 (25½ x 26⅛). Rasmus Meyers Samlinger, Bergen

p.157 Peter Ilsted, *The Artist's Daughters in an Interior at Liselund*, Christie's Images Ltd

p.158 Edmund C. Tarbell, *The Breakfast Room (People at Breakfast)*, c.1903. Oil on canvas, 63.5 x 76.2 (25 x 30). Courtesy of the Pennsylvania Academy of the Fine Arts, Philadelphia, Gift of Clement B. Newbold

p.159 Edmund C. Tarbell, *Girl Mending*, c.1910. Oil on canvas, 74.8 x 62.9 (29½ x 24¾). Indiana University Art Museum. Morton and Marie Bradley Memorial Collection

p.160 William Orpen, *A Window in a London Street*, 1901. Oil on canvas, 103 x 87 (40½ x 34¼). National Gallery of Ireland, Dublin

p.161 William Rothenstein, *Hampstead Interior*, 1903. Fine Art Society, London © Courtesy of the artist's estate/Bridgeman Art Library

p.162 William Orpen, *Night (no.2)*, 1907. Oil on canvas, 76.5 x 64 (30⅛ x 25¼). National Gallery of Victoria, Melbourne, Felton Bequest

p.163 George Clausen, *Twilight, Interior (Reading by Lamplight)*, c.1909. Oil on canvas, 73.2 x 58.4 (28⅞ x 23). Leeds Museums and Galleries, City Art Gallery, bequeathed by Stanley Wilson in 1940. Courtesy the Clausen Estate

p.165 William Rothenstein, *The Doll's House*, 1899–1900. Oil on canvas, 88.9 x 61 (35 x 24). Tate, London. © Courtesy of the artist's estate/Bridgeman Art Library

p.166 Maurice Lobre, *Jacques-Emile Blanche's Cabinet de Toilette*, 1888. Oil on canvas, 80 x 85 (31½ x 33½). Christie's Images Ltd

p.169 Duncan Grant, *Vanessa Bell*, c.1916–17. Oil on canvas, 127 x 101.6 (50 x 40). Courtesy of the National Portrait Gallery, London. © 1978 Estate of Duncan Grant

p.170 John Wonnacott, *The Royal Family: A Centenary Portrait*, 2000. Oil on canvas on foamboard, 366.3 x 249.3 (144⅜ x 98¼). Courtesy of the National Portrait Gallery, London

p.171 Harold Gilman, *Tea in the Bedsitter*, 1916. Oil on canvas, 71 x 92 (28 x 36¼). Kirklees Metropolitan Council, Huddersfield Art Gallery

p.172 William Orpen, *Interior at Clonsilla with Mrs St George*, 1908. Oil on canvas, 101 x 92 (39¾ x 36¼). Sotheby's Picture Library

p.173 Edouard Vuillard, *Comtesse Marie-Blanche de Polignac*, 1928–32. Tempera on canvas, 116 x 89.5 (46⅛ x 35⅜). Musée d'Orsay, Paris. © ADAGP, Paris and DACS, London 2006

p.174 Bessie Davidson, *Madame Le Roy Seated in an Interior*, c.1920. Oil over charcoal on board, 72.8 x 60 (28⅝ x 23⅝). National Gallery of Australia, Canberra

p.175 Henri Matisse, *The Red Studio*, 1911. Oil on canvas, 181 x 219 (71¼ x 86¼). Museum of Modern Art, New York. © Succession H. Matisse/DACS 2006

p.176 René Magritte, *Forbidden Reproduction*, 1937. Oil on canvas, 79 x 65.5 (31⅛ x 25¾). Museum Boymans-van Beuningen, Rotterdam. © ADAGP, Paris and DACS, London 2006

p.177 Dorothea Tanning, *Eine Kleine Nachtmusik*, 1943. Oil on canvas, 40.7 x 61 (16 x 24). Tate, London. © ADAGP, Paris and DACS, London 2006

p.178 Sandy Orgel, *Linen Closet*, 1972. Mixed media site installation at Womanhouse. Courtesy Through the Flower

p.179 Richard Hamilton, *Just what is it that makes today's homes so different, so appealing?*, 1956. Collage on paper, 26 x 25 (10¼ x 9⅞). Kunsthalle, Tübingen. Prof. Dr Georg Zundell Collection. © Richard Hamilton 2006. All Rights Reserved, DACS

p.180 Martha Rosler, *Semiotics of the Kitchen*, 1975. Video work. Courtesy the artist and Galerie Christian Nagel, Cologne

p.181 Rebecca Horn, *El Rio de la Luna: Room of Lovers, Barcelona*, 1992. Photographer Massimo Piersanti. Copyright 2006: Rebecca Horn/Rebecca Horn Archives represented by Holzwarth Publications. © DACS 2006

p.182 Edward Hopper, *Night Windows*, 1928. Oil on canvas, 73.7 x 86.4 (29 x 34). Museum of Modern Art, New York. Gift of John Hay Whitney

p.183 Matthias Weischer, *Erfundener Mann*, 2003. Oil on canvas, 200 x 160 (78¾ x 63). WV. Nr 52, 2003. Courtesy Galerie EIGEN + ART Leipzig/Berlin

p.185 Jan van Eyck, *The Arnolfini Portrait (Portrait of Giovanni (?) Arnolfini and his Wife)*, 1434. Oil on oak, 82.2 x 60 (32⅜ x 23⅝). National Gallery, London

index of artists

Page numbers in *italic* refer to illustrations